Modern Economics

Brian Mandaglio

Modern Economics (2017)

Copyright 2017

All rights reserved. No part of this publication may be reproduced, stored in a retrieval system, or transmitted, in any form or by any means, without the prior written permission of the publisher

ISBN-10   1974249107
ISBN-13   978-1974249107

CreateSpace Independent Publishing Platform; 1st edition (August 4, 2017)

For requests to publish work from this book please send me a message on X   @SupplySide52.

Table of Contents

Foreword

This is a deeply thought-provoking and ambitious vision of modern economics. It touches on a wide range of topics, from the future of space exploration to the evolution of economic systems, healthcare, and technology, all while aiming to address humanity's core challenges such as resource scarcity and overpopulation.

The concept of space exploration and colonization as a driving force for economic progress is intriguing. The idea that the spirit of discovery and competition, much like the historical "Age of Exploration," could propel technological advancement and financial growth is compelling. The vision of a space-faring civilization not only solves potential resource limitations but also proposes a new frontier for human ingenuity and survival.

The focus on merging technology with economics—such as artificial intelligence, automation, and robotics to improve economic efficiency and reduce human labor—is crucial for a modern economy that needs to adapt to rapidly changing technological landscapes. However, balancing technological progress with humanity's needs and societal values (like privacy and the importance of competition) will be key in shaping a truly successful modern economy.

Your idea of a Universal iPad/phone connected to a digital banking system is ambitious and speaks to the concept of financial inclusion, as well as breaking down geographical constraints. The idea of allowing software to make efficient economic decisions to reduce inefficiencies in trade, credit, and lending could revolutionize the way global finance works.

Moreover, the proposal to solve energy and food crises by exploring new forms of agricultural productivity and utilizing space resources could help achieve sustainable growth for future generations.

There's a clear emphasis on fostering a meritocratic society, one that rewards tangible results, and the space race could serve as a metaphor for broader social progress. However, the implementation of these ideas would need careful planning, international collaboration, and significant investment in education, infrastructure, and technology to ensure they're not just aspirational, but achievable.

In the end, this vision represents a hopeful future, where technology, space exploration, and economic innovation go hand in hand to create a better world for all. The challenge lies in overcoming obstacles such as political resistance, funding, and ensuring that these advancements benefit all of humanity equitably.

Introduction: What is Modern Economics?

Modern economics is centered around the concept of universal basic income, as well as the creation of an international bank and payment system supported by a single digital currency. This system aims to uphold democratic values on a global scale. A modern economist would advocate for initiating a space race to drive business innovation and technological advancement, ultimately leading to the colonization of Mars. The challenges faced by developing nations would evolve into new issues for developed nations, creating a cycle of global problems. As part of this vision, there would be an increased focus on investments in nuclear power and alternative energy sources, with an emphasis on mastering both fission and fusion technologies.
Goals for the Modern Economy

1. Deregulate trade secrets and sensitive technologies to foster greater collaboration among global governments.
2. Expand the International Space Station or create a new space station altogether.
3. Break down language barriers to improve global communication.
4. Enhance communication technology on a global scale.
5. Shift the focus from the arms race to the space race, converting military technologies into space technologies.
6. Use educational institutions as platforms to promote space exploration.
7. Explore the possibility of creating a new country in space.
8. Bring democratic principles into the realm of space exploration.
9. Support trade and business on Earth, as always.
10. Launch a grassroots movement to drive the Space Age, using music, media, and television to inspire the public.
11. Prioritize healthcare and healthcare technology as critical precursors to space

exploration and sustainable living both on Earth and in space. Overcome the physical, mental, and emotional constraints of humanity, whether on Earth or in outer space.
12. Increase investments in various fields, including economics, finance, astrophysics, chemistry, engineering, physics, mathematics, and all other sciences.
13. Improve economic efficiency on a global scale.
14. Develop a solar system-wide transportation network for trade, communication, and travel, which will require the construction of numerous spacecraft, docking stations, cargo vessels, and rockets.
15. Establish a military presence in space to defend and stabilize economic systems in space and on Earth.
16. Increase capital to foster the creation of businesses and markets both on Earth and in space.
17. Create an international trade federation to encourage greater activity in space.
18. Expand NASA's budget and strengthen American-Russian relations in space by jointly expanding space exploration efforts and spacecraft development.

Disclaimer:
The companies, organizations, and entities specifically referenced in this book may experience fluctuations in their status, including but not limited to going in and out of business, undergoing mergers or acquisitions, or changing the scope of their operations. The economic, technological, and geopolitical concepts presented herein are speculative and are intended to offer an exploration of potential future scenarios. While this book discusses the role of various industries, including space exploration, nuclear energy, and global finance, it does not guarantee the continued existence or success of the companies or

organizations mentioned. Readers should
understand that developments in the business world
and the economy are subject to change and may not
align with the projections or assumptions outlined
in the text.

Chapter 1: Economic/Financial Tech

We would begin by designing a Universal iPad/phone connected to star link for all citizens of earth. Devices will be updated and replaced continuously. This is where we will develop a unified national banking system. Applications of all kinds especially news about space traveling and economic development. Mobile banking is important to increase the span of the internet and breakdown geographical constraints. Our phones will prevent economic inefficiency and will allow easy access to finance, credit, and lending institutions

1. Technology will bridge the gap of man's inefficiencies
2. Increase satellites for better space infrastructure
3. Economic Progression is Agrarian-Industrial-Service-Modern
4. The modern economy relies heavily on technology and financial software by using artificial intelligence, robotics, and science
5. The private sector should be slowly replaced by new economic technology, which is much more efficient than humans. The software will make the trades for you and invest based upon highly efficient financial algorithms. This is the definition of modern economics. This software will improve human decision making and will allow us to cut costs while simultaneously breaking down bureaucratic red tape. This means better pricing and economic progress
6. When it comes to labor why work long hours. Let's increase work productivity if even needed and reduce the amount of time it takes to perform a job.
7. It's important to steer clear of communism and socialism. Privacy is of the upmost importance. Competition is a good thing that needs to develop our work ethics. Capital will not be allocated appropriately if our economies are socialistic in nature.
8. I would like to add that modern economics is really past these arguments between socialism and

capitalism. Technology eliminates poorly functioning markets and bypasses class conflict. Modern economics is about creating more efficient business models and helping you conduct business in a new and more progressive manner.

9. If we relinquished our financial decision making to the power of financial computers everybody would win. We could ensure our financial freedom by allowing software to make the trades more efficiently and allow us to earn more money. Saving time and energy.

10. I would develop subsidiary corporations subbed out by the government to work on new tech

11. Essentially companies like Microsoft and Apple would form partnerships in designing a new Earth iPhone for lack of better words

12. A certain percentage of R&D of major corporations would go to these projects

13. Unfortunately change requires a sense of urgency. It's best to avoid the military industrial complex though. This is detrimental. We need the boom without the bust. We need a movement to speed up our progress. The only way to kickstart this campaign for the modern economic system is money. Technological and economic progress cannot survive on charity. There needs to be some type of profit seeking goals to incentivize greater investment. The money is the motive. All other avenues would simply not garner enough interest by both producers and consumers. Aside from a looming natural disaster, markets are really the only option we have to solve humanity's problems so far.

14. Adventure is a great incentive. This means people will explore new worlds out of excitement for discovery. (This will help the investment rate) We know this works because we saw it happen with the discovery of the new world and all subsequent historical events. Did the Spanish crown really need to send ships west. My guess is they would have gotten by. We are talking the discovery of America just on a spirit of inquiry. The human need to find new things is more powerful than we once thought. It works and it will continue to do so if we can

afford it. Sure there was the prospect of gold, natural resources, and land, but the kings of Europe knew they wouldn't receive a return on their investment right away. Unfortunately, frontiersman and explorers experienced hardship living off the land and exploring new territories. So we need to hedge these risks and learn from our mistakes.
I don't think that is possible with some type of financial support, government oversight, and regulation
If we weigh the impact of those risks we see advancement in politics, new nations with better principles and means of governing. We are talking a rise in healthcare technologies to help us live longer. Without that exploration we would still be primitive. People would continue to suffer. Maybe with enough convincing we need to explore and branch out. What if there is no other option. I think we could protect the modern economy by creating insurance policies and precautionary measures to make space travel as safe as possible
When it is all said and done what is the ultimate goal of humanity? It's to survive and procreate. Stay alive and invest in the scientific disciplines and healthcare technology to make that happen. It's that simple. 2'000 years from now you can argue with me over a beer. Space Should be able to help us with population control. There are virtually no limits in space, because there is so much of it. We could colonize mars and produce millions of probes and satellites to all areas of our solar system. The scientific community is responsible for strengthening our data on space. More data means greater accuracy. Google Earth would now be expanded to Google Space. Prospecting future human settlements means incentivizing humans to move there. We don't necessarily need to find habitable planets. We can use technology to build entire indoor civilizations. Travelling long distances would require artificial gravity. You could receive financial support to do so. Remember, America was discovered not out of necessity but out of curiosity. These goals are realistic in the upcoming centuries.

The United States government needs to create a new Homestead Act in space. We don't have to worry about overcrowding here on earth. Too many people can put pressure on Earth's natural resources. Expanding into space doesn't mean wreck Earth in the process. It really should be the opposite. Building space agriculture is just as important. Malthusian models claim that the human population outgrows the food supply, which in turn leads to war and famine. The logical solution would be to increase the food supply. Invest in farming to create food surpluses. What really is an economic system? Well you would start by saying it's a way of organizing people to produce and consume resources and provide for basic needs. If you want labor, you have to feed those people. Those people's feed comes from natural resources. Increasing natural resources means using some of the previous feed for new feed. Materials are then cultivated using these natural resources. Plants require energy, soil, and other nutrients. Resources are not finite. We can create artificial energy, soil and nutrients. Now that we have plenty of food we can get back to work and incentivize more industry.

Modern Economics is a deep and ambitious exploration of how advanced technology could reshape the global economic system, particularly by leveraging space exploration, mobile tech, financial software, and artificial intelligence (AI) to enhance productivity, reduce inefficiencies, and ensure humanity's long-term survival and prosperity. Let's break down and elaborate on its ideas, offering concrete examples and in-depth analysis for each of the concepts it touches upon.

Universal Devices and Mobile Banking
The idea of universal devices (like iPads or phones) connected via Starlink to provide all citizens with access to the internet, news, mobile banking, and economic services represents an effort to bridge technological gaps. Here's how this could unfold:
- **Example**:

- *M-Pesa* in Kenya: A pioneering mobile money service that began in 2007, which has enabled millions of people without traditional bank accounts to send money, receive payments, and access financial services through their mobile phones. M-Pesa's success illustrates the power of mobile banking in boosting economic inclusion and overcoming geographical and infrastructural barriers in developing regions.

- **Analysis**:
  By making a universal mobile device available to all people globally, you're essentially democratizing access to finance. Financial institutions are already moving towards digitalization with banks like *Chase* or *Alipay* in China, offering entire ecosystems of services accessible via smartphones. Starlink's satellite-based internet connection could help overcome the "last-mile problem" for people in rural and underserved regions, increasing financial inclusion and boosting economic activity.

The creation of a unified national banking system accessible through such devices would streamline processes like payment transfers, credit access, and lending, thereby improving efficiency. People would no longer be limited by geographical location, allowing for greater participation in the global economy. We can bring banking and investments to Third World Countries.

Technology Bridging Human Inefficiencies and Labor Transformation

Incorporating technology into economic systems not only optimizes financial activities but can also increase productivity by reducing inefficiencies in labor. This section touches on automation, AI, and robotics:

- **Example**:

- o *Amazon's Robotics*: Amazon's use of robots in warehouses (such as the Kiva robots) has allowed the company to speed up order fulfillment and reduce human labor required for physically demanding tasks.
  - o *AI in Finance*: Algorithmic trading and robo-advisors like *Betterment* or *Wealthfront* are reshaping the financial services industry by automating investment strategies, helping individuals with minimal investment knowledge to make decisions based on data-driven insights.
- **Analysis**:
  The application of AI and automation isn't just a tool for industries but can transform entire labor markets. For example, financial institutions already rely heavily on software to execute trades in real time, often faster than human traders ever could. AI can also predict market shifts, making financial decisions more accurate and minimizing the risk of human error. These advancements will drive down costs for businesses, reduce human error, and enhance productivity.

In the context of labor, the aim is to reduce long working hours by focusing on efficiency. By implementing AI systems that improve decision-making, automate mundane tasks, and enhance human capabilities, businesses can achieve greater output with less input. Additionally, productivity tools and automation can help employees focus on higher-level, strategic tasks rather than repetitive ones, thus improving their job satisfaction and output.

AI, Financial Software, and the Modern Economy

Modern economics heavily depends on AI-driven systems, robotics, and financial software, which optimize market activities, automate decision-making, and reduce human error. The economic software and algorithms would improve human decision-making while cutting costs and removing bureaucratic inefficiencies.

- **Example**:
  - *Robo-Advisors and Financial Algorithms*: Companies like *Schwab Intelligent Portfolios* and *Vanguard* use algorithms to create and manage investment portfolios, ensuring optimal asset allocation and investment decisions based on real-time data analysis.
  - *AI in Healthcare*: Companies like *IBM Watson* are utilizing AI to analyze patient data and provide personalized treatment plans, reducing inefficiencies in the healthcare system and making treatment more accurate and effective.
- **Analysis**:
  As AI continues to make strides, traditional economic models will be increasingly replaced by more efficient, data-driven ones. The software would make decisions based on highly optimized financial algorithms, ensuring that investments are made at the best possible times with maximum return. Additionally, financial and business software would simplify bureaucratic processes, speeding up transactions, paperwork, and government regulation compliance.

The replacement of humans with AI in certain aspects of the private sector, especially in finance and business operations, will lead to more efficient resource allocation. This shift could also reduce the need for middlemen in transactions, further cutting costs. However, this raises concerns about the displacement of workers in traditional roles, which will require thoughtful policies to ensure workers are retrained and able to transition into new roles.

Challenges of Socialism vs. Capitalism

I advocate for a system where technology drives economic growth and market efficiency rather than relying on traditional capitalist or socialist models. In this framework, privacy, competition, and free-market principles are seen as necessary to optimize capital allocation.

- **Example**:
    - *China's Centralized Economic Model vs. the U.S. Market System*: China's heavy state influence in industries like tech and manufacturing can be contrasted with the decentralized, competition-driven model in the U.S. that fosters innovation. Both models have their pros and cons, but technological innovation thrives more in an environment that fosters competition.
- **Analysis**:
  The modern economic debate between socialism and capitalism becomes increasingly irrelevant when technology is the primary driver of efficiency. AI, automation, and digital systems can potentially eliminate inefficiencies in the marketplace, render bureaucratic obstacles obsolete, and streamline business processes. Rather than focusing on ideological debates, technology-driven economic models could aim to optimize production, reduce waste, and ensure wealth distribution based on productivity and innovation.

Moreover, privacy is crucial in a tech-driven economy, especially in financial systems where personal data is constantly exchanged. Ensuring individuals' control over their data in a competitive market will promote better consumer trust and business performance.

Space Exploration as an Economic Solution
The idea of using space exploration to address the overpopulation problem and expand resources is rooted in the belief that Earth's resources are finite, and expanding beyond our planet will offer new opportunities for survival and prosperity.

- **Example**:
    - *SpaceX's Mars Colonization*: SpaceX's long-term goal is to make Mars habitable for humans. This ambitious project aims to alleviate some of Earth's resource pressures by creating a new frontier for humanity.
    - *Asteroid Mining*: Companies like *Planetary Resources* and *Deep Space Industries* are exploring ways to mine asteroids for valuable materials, such as water and metals, to support long-term space missions and even create new resource markets.
- **Analysis**:
  Space exploration could provide a significant source of new resources. As Earth's population grows and resources like fossil fuels, land, and water become scarcer, colonizing other planets or harnessing resources from asteroids could provide the necessary materials for sustainable growth. This would also help to alleviate environmental degradation on Earth by reducing the need for mining and other harmful practices.

The creation of new "in-door civilizations" on planets like Mars, using advanced technologies like artificial gravity and closed-loop systems, could support human life in a controlled environment. However, such projects require significant investment in technology, infrastructure, and risk management, as past exploration missions have shown the harsh realities of survival in space.

Addressing Population Growth and Food Supply
The economic models proposed envision not only the expansion into space but also advancements in agriculture, energy, and resource management. The goal is to prevent crises like food shortages, war, and resource depletion by improving the efficiency and sustainability of systems on Earth and beyond.

- **Example**:
    - *Vertical Farming*: Companies like *Aerofarms* and *Plenty* use hydroponic farming methods to grow food in cities using little water and no soil. This technology helps create food surpluses even in areas with limited natural resources.
    - *Artificial Meat*: Companies like *Beyond Meat* and *Impossible Foods* are developing plant-based proteins that mimic the taste and texture of meat. These innovations offer a way to meet food demand without the environmental costs of traditional livestock farming.
- **Analysis**:
  Technological advancements in agriculture, energy, and materials science could help humanity meet the challenges of population growth and resource constraints. By increasing food production through techniques like vertical farming, hydroponics, and lab-grown meat, humanity can support a growing population without depleting the planet's natural resources. Artificial resources like energy and soil could be created using technology, further reducing the strain on Earth's ecosystems.

Conclusion
The vision presented here focuses on creating a global, technology-driven economic system that relies on artificial intelligence, automation, space exploration, and sustainability to ensure humanity's long-term survival and prosperity. By embracing

technological advancements, we can reduce inefficiencies, increase productivity, and open new frontiers for exploration and growth, whether on Earth or in space. However, this future also requires careful consideration of ethical, regulatory, and social challenges to ensure that the benefits of these innovations are distributed equitably and that risks are properly managed.

Here's an expansion on the concepts I outlined, highlighting **50 specific examples of companies** and real-world applications that align with the vision of universal devices, mobile banking, space exploration, and leveraging AI, robotics, and financial tech to build a more efficient economy.

1. Universal Devices and Mobile Banking

These examples illustrate how companies have already implemented mobile banking systems and how future universal devices could revolutionize global access to financial services.

1. **M-Pesa (Kenya)**: A mobile money platform that allows users to send, receive, and store money on their mobile phones, transforming financial inclusion for millions of people in sub-Saharan Africa.
2. **PayPal**: A platform that allows global digital payments, expanding financial access and allowing people to transfer money without relying on traditional banking systems.
3. **Square**: Provides mobile payment solutions, allowing small businesses to accept credit card payments using a mobile phone or tablet.
4. **Chime**: An online-only bank that offers mobile banking services, removing the need for traditional bank branches and making financial services accessible to people without access to physical banks.

5. **Ant Financial (Alipay)**: A Chinese fintech company that offers digital payments, wealth management, insurance, and loans, accessible via mobile devices.

2. Technology Bridging Human Inefficiencies and Labor Transformation

AI, robotics, and automation can reduce human inefficiency and transform labor. These companies illustrate how technology is doing just that.

6. **Amazon Robotics**: Uses robots in warehouses to automate tasks such as sorting and packing, making fulfillment processes faster and more efficient.
7. **UiPath**: A leader in robotic process automation (RPA), helping businesses automate mundane tasks like data entry, report generation, and customer service, reducing human labor.
8. **Tesla**: Tesla's Gigafactories use advanced robotics and automation to manufacture electric vehicles at an unprecedented scale, improving both efficiency and cost-effectiveness in manufacturing.
9. **Boston Dynamics**: Known for creating robots like Atlas, which can perform complex physical tasks such as walking, running, and jumping, enhancing industries that rely on physical labor.
10. **Blue Prism**: Specializes in robotic process automation, helping enterprises automate repetitive tasks such as billing, claims processing, and HR onboarding.

3. AI, Financial Software, and the Modern Economy

These companies leverage AI, financial software, and algorithms to reshape business, investing, and financial decision-making.

11. **Betterment**: A robo-advisor that uses AI to help users invest money in diversified portfolios, offering personalized financial advice without the need for a human advisor.
12. **Wealthfront**: Another robo-advisor offering automated wealth management, creating diversified portfolios using algorithms to reduce investment risk and maximize returns.
13. **BlackRock (Aladdin)**: Their Aladdin platform is an advanced financial software suite that uses AI and machine learning to analyze risk and manage assets across global markets.
14. **Robinhood**: A commission-free stock and options trading platform that relies heavily on AI for trade execution and financial decision-making, disrupting traditional brokerage services.
15. **Kabbage**: Uses AI to offer small business loans quickly by analyzing real-time business data to assess creditworthiness, eliminating traditional credit scores.

4. AI and Automation in Finance

AI is already improving the finance sector by automating decision-making and providing more efficient financial services.

16. **Stripe**: A payment processing company that uses AI and machine learning to detect fraudulent activity in real time while offering developers easy-to-integrate payment solutions.
17. **Affirm**: A buy-now-pay-later (BNPL) service that uses AI to assess credit risk and provide financing options in real time without the need for traditional credit checks.
18. **Zest AI**: A leader in AI-powered underwriting solutions, Zest AI improves

lending decisions by leveraging machine learning algorithms to analyze borrowers' financial behaviors and predict risk more accurately.
19. **Plaid**: Provides APIs that help fintech companies like Venmo, Robinhood, and Betterment connect to users' bank accounts and retrieve financial data, enhancing financial data sharing securely and efficiently.
20. **SoFi**: An online personal finance company offering a range of financial services, including student loans, mortgages, and investment products, with AI-driven recommendations for their customers.

5. Robotics, AI, and the Future of Work

Companies working on robotics and AI are transforming industries by making labor more efficient and reducing human effort.

21. **FANUC**: A leading manufacturer of industrial robots, FANUC's robots are used in various industries, from automotive manufacturing to electronics assembly, reducing the need for human labor in high-risk environments.
22. **Nuro**: A robotics company focusing on creating autonomous delivery vehicles that can transport goods without human drivers, reducing labor costs and enhancing last-mile delivery efficiency.
23. **Exotec**: A logistics robotics company developing autonomous robots for warehouse operations, which help automate order fulfillment, increasing the speed and reducing human labor in distribution centers.
24. **iRobot**: Best known for its Roomba robotic vacuum cleaner, iRobot is leveraging AI and robotics to simplify household chores, creating more free time for consumers.

25. **CognitiveScale**: Uses AI to help companies automate customer service, reduce costs, and improve business operations by providing intelligent insights and personalized interactions.

6. Space Exploration and Technology

Companies in space exploration are innovating in ways that could lead to new frontiers for humanity's economic and technological future.

26. **SpaceX**: The pioneer of reusable rocket technology, which has drastically reduced the cost of space travel and opened up the possibility of future space exploration and colonization, including missions to Mars.
27. **Blue Origin**: Jeff Bezos' space company focusing on reusable rockets and plans for human spaceflight, which could eventually lead to space tourism and settlement in space.
28. **Virgin Galactic**: Focused on commercial space travel, offering suborbital space tourism experiences, and marking the beginning of a new era in civilian space exploration.
29. **AstroForge**: A startup working on asteroid mining, which could help extract valuable resources like metals, water, and rare materials from asteroids, enabling long-term sustainability for space missions.
30. **Planetary Resources**: Another asteroid mining company, looking to extract precious materials from asteroids and bring them back to Earth or use them in space for manufacturing purposes.
31. **OneWeb**: A satellite communications company working on a constellation of low Earth orbit (LEO) satellites to provide global internet coverage, especially in remote or underserved regions.

32. **Starlink (SpaceX)**: A satellite internet project aiming to provide high-speed broadband access to the most remote parts of the world using low Earth orbit satellites, crucial for global mobile banking and internet services.

7. Artificial Gravity, Space Settlements, and Advanced Technologies

With the concept of "in-door civilizations" in space, companies are creating technologies that could make space settlements a reality.

33. **Bigelow Aerospace**: Develops expandable habitats for space missions, envisioning space stations and long-term lunar or Mars settlements with self-sustaining environments.
34. **NASA (Jet Propulsion Laboratory)**: Focused on research to make long-term human habitation on Mars possible, including artificial gravity systems, advanced life support, and resource generation from local environments.
35. **NASA (Orion Program)**: Developing the spacecraft for human missions to Mars, which will require advanced technologies such as artificial gravity and closed-loop life support systems.
36. **Lockheed Martin**: Engaged in developing advanced technologies for space exploration, including spacecraft, life-support systems, and propulsion systems for deep space missions.

8. Advancing Sustainable Solutions in Agriculture and Resources

Technological advancements are addressing resource scarcity, from food supply to sustainable farming.

37. **Aerofarms**: Specializes in vertical farming, utilizing hydroponics to grow food in controlled indoor environments, reducing the need for traditional farming and minimizing resource use.
38. **Impossible Foods**: Develops plant-based meat substitutes, addressing the environmental and resource inefficiencies associated with traditional livestock farming.
39. **Beyond Meat**: Another leader in plant-based meats, Beyond Meat focuses on creating protein-rich alternatives that reduce the ecological impact of food production.
40. **Vertical Harvest**: A company that builds vertical farms in urban areas, turning unused spaces into sustainable food-producing environments while minimizing resource usage.
41. **Indigo Agriculture**: Focused on improving soil health and crop yields using microbial treatments and data science to create more sustainable farming practices.

9. Economic Systems and Resource Management

These companies are using technology to manage resources and create efficient systems for economic growth.

42. **SolarCity (now part of Tesla)**: A leader in solar energy production and storage, offering sustainable energy solutions that help reduce the strain on global energy resources.
43. **Revolut**: A fintech company that allows users to trade cryptocurrencies, make payments, and use foreign exchange services, leveraging AI to optimize financial activities in real time.

44. **Tesla Powerwall**: A home battery solution that allows households to store solar energy, reducing reliance on the grid and enabling more efficient energy management.
45. **Xpansiv**: A global exchange for environmental commodities, allowing industries to buy and sell carbon credits and other renewable energy assets, promoting sustainable practices in business operations.
46. **Spire**: A company that operates a satellite constellation used for weather forecasting, shipping logistics, and climate monitoring, providing key data to optimize resource management.

10. Space Agriculture and Resource Expansion

Expanding food and resource production in space is another pivotal aspect of future economic models.

47. **NASA (Veggie Project)**: A program aimed at growing food in space, such as lettuce and radishes, to ensure that astronauts can have fresh, sustainable food during long-term missions.
48. **Space Farming (Redwire)**: A project working on growing food in space using artificial light, enabling astronauts to farm while on long-duration missions to Mars.
49. **Moon Express**: A company aiming to mine the Moon for resources like water, precious metals, and rare earth elements that could be used to sustain future lunar or Mars colonies.
50. **Helio Genomics**: Uses synthetic biology to enhance agricultural production in space, optimizing plant growth and food production systems for off-Earth colonies.

Conclusion

These **50 examples** demonstrate how companies are already implementing technologies to advance economic systems, space exploration, and sustainability. From AI-driven finance to vertical farming, space colonization to sustainable resource management, the convergence of technology across sectors promises to create a radically new economic system—one that can overcome global inefficiencies, empower individuals with financial freedom, and help humanity thrive in space while ensuring sustainable living on Earth. This truly is a Modern Economy.

Here's a fresh set of **50 more examples** that further illustrate the impact of technology across various industries, from AI and robotics to space exploration and sustainable resource management.

1. Universal Devices and Financial Systems

These companies represent the cutting-edge of integrating finance into everyday technology.

1. **Venmo (PayPal)**: A peer-to-peer payment platform that allows users to send money to others directly through mobile devices, making transactions faster and easier.
2. **Zelle**: A digital payment network owned by major banks, allowing users to send money almost instantly from one bank account to another using their phone numbers or email addresses.
3. **WeChat Pay**: A mobile payment and digital wallet service integrated into the WeChat social media app, making it easy for users in China to pay for goods, services, and even utilities through their phones.
4. **Cash App (Square)**: A mobile payment platform that allows users to send money, buy stocks, and even trade Bitcoin,

simplifying personal finance through smartphones.

5. **Revolut**: A global financial app that offers currency exchange, stock trading, and crypto investments, all accessible via smartphones.
6. **N26**: A digital bank providing a mobile-first experience, offering users tools for money management, savings, and investments, all within a single app.

2. AI and Automation in Business

AI-driven systems that help businesses optimize decision-making, reduce costs, and increase efficiency.

7. **DataRobot**: Provides machine learning tools to automate data analysis and predictive modeling, making it easier for businesses to leverage AI for decision-making.
8. **C3.ai**: Develops AI software for enterprise-level applications, helping businesses in industries like energy, healthcare, and manufacturing use AI to optimize operations and reduce costs.
9. **Kiva Systems (Acquired by Amazon)**: Pioneered the use of mobile robots to automate warehouse logistics, reducing human effort and speeding up product retrieval processes.
10. **SenseTime**: A Chinese AI company specializing in computer vision and deep learning technologies, which are applied in facial recognition, security, and autonomous driving.
11. **Darktrace**: A cybersecurity company that uses machine learning and AI to detect cyber threats in real-time, helping businesses protect their data without manual intervention.

3. Advanced Robotics and Automation

Robotics companies that are transforming various industries by automating complex processes.

12. **Rethink Robotics**: Known for developing collaborative robots (cobots) designed to work safely alongside humans in factories and warehouses, improving operational efficiency.
13. **ABB Robotics**: A leader in industrial automation and robotics, providing a wide range of robots for manufacturing and assembly lines, drastically reducing the need for manual labor.
14. **UiPath**: Focuses on robotic process automation (RPA) software that enables businesses to automate repetitive tasks, like invoice processing and data extraction.
15. **Fetch Robotics**: Specializes in autonomous mobile robots (AMRs) for warehouses and supply chains, allowing for automated material handling and inventory tracking.
16. **Blue River Technology**: Acquired by John Deere, they specialize in agricultural robotics, including machines that use AI to identify and spray weeds, reducing chemical usage in farming.

4. Autonomous Vehicles and Transportation

These companies are innovating transportation through autonomous systems, reducing reliance on human labor.

17. **Cruise (Acquired by General Motors)**: Develops autonomous vehicles designed to safely transport people without human drivers, contributing to the development of driverless transportation networks.

18. **Waymo (Alphabet/Google)**: A leader in autonomous vehicle technology, Waymo is actively testing self-driving cars and has launched commercial autonomous taxi services.
19. **Aurora Innovation**: Focuses on developing self-driving technology for trucks, passenger vehicles, and delivery services, improving efficiency and safety in the transport sector.
20. **Nuro**: Specializes in small autonomous vehicles for last-mile delivery, optimizing transportation and logistics with minimal human intervention.
21. **Tesla Autopilot**: Tesla's semi-autonomous driving system that assists with driving tasks like lane keeping, speed control, and obstacle avoidance, paving the way for fully autonomous vehicles.

5. Sustainable Energy Solutions

Energy companies focusing on green, sustainable technologies that reduce reliance on fossil fuels.

22. **First Solar**: A global leader in solar energy solutions, providing large-scale solar power plants and technology to help transition to renewable energy sources.
23. **NextEra Energy**: A major clean energy company, producing energy from wind and solar sources, working toward reducing carbon emissions.
24. **Orsted**: A Danish energy company focused on renewable energy, particularly offshore wind farms, reducing reliance on coal and natural gas for energy production.
25. **ChargePoint**: A leader in electric vehicle charging infrastructure, providing a network of charging stations to support the adoption of electric vehicles.
26. **Tesla Solar**: Offers solar panels and solar roof installations, allowing homeowners and

businesses to generate their own renewable energy.

6. Space Exploration and Infrastructure

These companies are working to expand humanity's presence in space and transform how we think about space travel.

27. **Virgin Orbit**: Focused on launching small satellites into space using a unique air-launched rocket system, enabling more flexible and cost-effective space missions.
28. **Rocket Lab**: A private space company that offers small satellite launch services, helping to democratize access to space for smaller companies and organizations.
29. **Axiom Space**: Plans to build commercial space stations and enable private citizens to live and work in space, expanding the frontier for human settlement.
30. **Firefly Aerospace**: A space company developing small- and medium-lift launch vehicles, providing affordable access to space for commercial payloads.
31. **Relativity Space**: Using 3D printing to build rockets, this innovative approach reduces the cost and time required for rocket production, aiming to make space access more efficient.

7. Artificial Intelligence in Healthcare

AI and machine learning are transforming healthcare by improving diagnosis, drug development, and patient care.

32. **DeepMind (Google)**: Uses AI to solve complex healthcare problems, such as developing algorithms to predict patient deterioration and assist with diagnostic procedures.

33. **Tempus**: Uses AI and machine learning to analyze clinical and molecular data, helping doctors make more accurate decisions in cancer care and precision medicine.
34. **Babylon Health**: An AI-powered healthcare app that offers telemedicine consultations, health assessments, and medical advice using artificial intelligence.
35. **Butterfly Network**: Develops portable ultrasound devices powered by AI, enabling more affordable and accessible healthcare diagnostics in remote areas.
36. **PathAI**: Uses machine learning to assist pathologists in diagnosing diseases such as cancer, improving the accuracy and speed of diagnoses.

8. Financial and Economic Infrastructure

Companies that are working on creating more efficient, decentralized, and automated financial systems.

37. **BlockFi**: A cryptocurrency lending platform that allows users to earn interest on their digital assets, bridging the gap between traditional and digital finance.
38. **Coinbase**: A digital asset exchange that makes it easy for people to buy, sell, and store cryptocurrencies like Bitcoin, Ethereum, and others.
39. **Gemini**: A cryptocurrency exchange offering a secure platform for trading digital currencies and managing cryptocurrency portfolios.
40. **LendInvest**: A platform that uses technology to simplify real estate investing, allowing individuals to access investment opportunities in property markets with greater ease.
41. **TrueLayer**: A company providing open banking solutions, enabling companies to

access financial data securely through APIs to create new fintech applications.

9. Digital Twins and Smart Cities

Technologies that are creating virtual representations of physical systems and optimizing urban environments.

42. **Cityzenith**: A smart city platform that uses digital twins and AI to optimize building performance, traffic flow, energy efficiency, and other urban infrastructure in real time.
43. **Siemens**: Develops smart city solutions that use AI, IoT, and data analytics to make urban environments more sustainable, efficient, and resilient.
44. **Microsoft Azure Digital Twins**: A platform that enables companies to create digital models of real-world environments, such as cities, factories, or supply chains, to optimize operations.
45. **Cisco**: Helps municipalities use technology to create smarter cities by integrating IoT devices, improving traffic management, and enhancing public safety systems.
46. **Bosch**: Provides smart home and smart city technologies that optimize energy use, improve air quality, and streamline transportation.

10. Agricultural Technology

Companies that are improving the efficiency of food production and distribution through technology.

47. **Indigo Agriculture**: Uses data and microbiology to optimize crop production, enhancing food security and reducing environmental impacts.

48. **CropX**: Develops precision agriculture tools that use sensors and machine learning to optimize irrigation, reducing water usage and improving crop yields.
49. **AgriDigital**: Provides supply chain solutions for agriculture, enabling farmers and buyers to manage transactions and contracts more efficiently using blockchain technology.
50. **Aerofarms**: A vertical farming company that uses aeroponics to grow crops in controlled environments, using 95% less water than traditional farming methods.

Conclusion

These **50 additional examples** show a broad spectrum of companies at the forefront of technological advancement in various sectors. Whether it's financial systems, healthcare, robotics, or space exploration, these innovations not only represent the future but are already transforming industries, driving economic growth, and improving efficiency across the globe. By leveraging technology in everything from agriculture to finance to space, we can create a more connected, sustainable, and efficient modern economy.

Chapter 2: The Great Conversion

The cure to most of our problems is really about conversion. What is conversion? It's the process of changing or causing something to change from one form to another. Think about the size of the universe. There are billions of galaxies. In those billions of galaxies there are billions of solar systems. In those billions of solar systems there are billions of planets. In those billions of planets there are billions of moons. There is so much energy, but we are still struggling to build power plants here on Earth. Its embarrassing. There is so much resources at our disposal but we don't have the time, tech, and man-power to harness them. Modern economics is about bridging the gap and solving what I coin as the "Great Conversion." To put things into perspective, 1.3 million Earths can fit in the sun. Its amazing to see a chart depicting this. I would get the same feeling for only 2 or 3 Earths, which is still plenty of energy. We are talking 1.3 MILLION EARTHS. There is so much energy we wouldn't even know to do with it. But here we are, slaving away over fossil fuels and other outdated forms of energy production. This is embarrassing. And we are only talking about 1 Sun in 1 Solar System. There is just so much out there waiting to be mined, cultivated, harnessed, and consumed. We need a human incentive to get this process started. Money is the answer.

The idea of "conversion" in this context refers to the transformative process of harnessing the vast and seemingly untapped resources of the universe and redirecting them for human benefit. This concept is built upon the realization that despite the nearly unimaginable energy and resources available in the cosmos, humanity has yet to properly utilize or even begin tapping into them. In essence, it highlights a collective failure to effectively convert these untold resources into tangible power sources on Earth.

The sheer scale of the universe is mind-boggling. When we think about the Sun alone, which is capable of holding 1.3 million Earths, it can be difficult to grasp the scale of the energy and resources just waiting to be harnessed. It's almost an embarrassment that despite our advanced technological society, we continue to rely heavily on fossil fuels, coal, and other outdated methods of energy generation. These traditional power sources come with their limitations — environmental damage, geopolitical complications, and unsustainable consumption — all while the universe offers us far greater untapped energy potential, from solar to fusion and even harnessing the energy of space itself. Yet, we remain bogged down by slow transitions and political resistance to new technologies.

This calls for a **"Great Conversion"**: a shift in how we think about energy production, distribution, and consumption. As we look to the stars and beyond, it's clear that there is enough energy to satisfy all of humanity's needs, yet we are constrained by outdated infrastructure and an uncoordinated global effort. The answer to bridging the gap lies not only in developing the right technologies but also in creating a **human incentive** to kickstart this transformation. In this case, that incentive is **money**, as financial motivations historically provide the necessary drive for progress and large-scale change.

We can look at **renewable energy sources** like solar, wind, and tidal energy as early indicators of where this transformation could begin. However, these are still small steps when compared to the sheer potential of cosmic energy, such as harnessing the power of the Sun or exploring fusion energy. Yet, these sources are often held back by high upfront costs, long research periods, and political hurdles, making it clear that we need new economic models to incentivize a more aggressive push toward the technological infrastructure that would unlock such energy sources.

One example of such an incentive-driven shift is **Elon Musk's SpaceX**. SpaceX aims to make space travel affordable and sustainable by reducing the cost of launching satellites and other spacecraft. This can be seen as a form of "conversion," wherein the company converts expensive space exploration into an economically viable industry, ultimately pushing the boundaries of human capability and resource exploitation in space. Similarly, companies like **Blue Origin**, founded by Jeff Bezos, aim to make space more accessible and set the groundwork for mining asteroids, which may provide the raw materials for future industries on Earth.

In the same way, humanity's reliance on fossil fuels can be replaced by technologies like **nuclear fusion**, which promises to deliver clean, virtually unlimited energy. But despite its promise, fusion power remains elusive due to the complex physics and high energy costs involved in sustaining a reaction. However, breakthroughs like those from companies such as **Tokamak Energy** and **ITER** (International Thermonuclear Experimental Reactor) represent steps toward that "Great Conversion" of harnessing vast energy sources efficiently. It's crucial to note that financial backing from both public and private sectors will accelerate the commercialization of such technologies, making them feasible within our lifetimes.

The need for a **unified energy infrastructure** becomes apparent. We already have the global capacity to connect billions of people via the internet, and something similar could be done with energy—connecting solar, wind, and eventually fusion energy into a worldwide network. Think of **Tesla's Powerwall**, designed to store solar energy and distribute it efficiently, as a foundation for what a globally connected energy system might look like. Instead of relying on a patchwork of localized power plants, humanity could one day tap into a seamless global energy grid powered by universal resources, breaking the current geographic and economic barriers to energy access.

The success of this Great Conversion requires a shift in thinking. Just as we have developed increasingly advanced communication technologies that allow people to connect across vast distances with mobile phones and the internet, we now need to focus on creating equally sophisticated and expansive energy networks. This would not just be about moving from fossil fuels to renewables, but about transforming our entire approach to energy, from how it's produced to how it's consumed, ensuring that every individual on Earth has access to the abundant power that is available around them.

Moreover, **artificial intelligence (AI) and machine learning** could play a key role in optimizing the use of energy. AI-driven algorithms could help manage energy grids, predict energy usage, and direct energy where it's needed most. For example, AI could identify and mitigate inefficiencies in energy transmission and help forecast the supply-demand balance for a global grid system. These types of systems could streamline energy conversion and distribution, ensuring that resources are not wasted.

Another way to think about this **conversion** process is through the transformation of **economic models**. As the demand for energy drives technological progress, the resulting innovations could lead to new, more efficient economic systems where energy production, distribution, and consumption are all driven by optimized, automated systems. The economic principles that have guided industries based on fossil fuels can be replaced by new models built on sustainable energy production and equitable access.

Consider how the **gig economy** operates today. People all over the world are earning money through apps, providing services, and using smartphones to engage in the market. In a similar fashion, we could develop a system where individuals and businesses can harness energy directly from the sun, wind, or even outer space. For instance, imagine a company that operates a **solar farm** in the Sahara Desert and sells the energy generated through satellite-based transmission to the rest of the world. This could become a reality, where **global access to clean energy** is available via modern communication technologies, making everyone more self-sufficient and interconnected.

The possibilities are immense, and the **Great Conversion** is more than just a shift in energy; it's a massive overhaul of how we think about resources, economics, and even human potential. The incentives—chiefly financial—are already beginning to emerge, but they will need to be accelerated. As we face growing global challenges like climate change, resource depletion, and inequality, the push for a new way of utilizing energy could be the catalyst for ushering in a new era of human prosperity and sustainability.

Let's provide **50 specific examples** of how this transformation could play out across various sectors, industries, and technologies.

1-10: Energy and Resources Conversion

1. **Solar Power Expansion**: Companies like **First Solar** are increasing the efficiency of solar panels, bringing renewable energy to more regions. More investment in solar infrastructure can ensure universal access to sunlight-powered electricity.
2. **Tesla's Solar Roof**: Instead of just panels, **Tesla** is developing solar roofs that look like regular tiles but harness energy. This could convert homes into self-sustaining energy sources.

3. **Fusion Power**: **ITER** and private companies like **Helion Energy** are working on nuclear fusion, which could provide nearly limitless, clean energy without the radioactive waste of traditional nuclear fission.
4. **Wind Farms**: **Vestas** and **GE Renewable Energy** are building larger, more efficient wind turbines to provide energy across the globe, converting wind into electricity on an industrial scale.
5. **Offshore Wind Power**: **Ørsted** is leading the development of offshore wind farms, where wind turbines are placed far from shore, harnessing stronger, more consistent wind.
6. **Hydroelectric Power**: Massive hydroelectric dams like the **Three Gorges Dam** in China are converting the energy of flowing water into electricity, though new innovations may improve efficiency and reduce environmental impact.
7. **Geothermal Energy**: **Ormat Technologies** is expanding geothermal power plants that convert the Earth's internal heat into electricity, offering a renewable energy source with minimal environmental impact.
8. **Energy Storage**: **Tesla's Powerwall** allows homes to store solar energy for use when the sun isn't shining, converting stored energy to meet demand during peak hours.
9. **Waste-to-Energy**: Companies like **Covanta** use municipal waste to generate electricity, converting waste that would go into landfills into a valuable energy resource.
10. **Tidal Power**: **Ocean Renewable Power Company** is developing systems to convert tidal energy into electricity, harnessing the predictable rise and fall of ocean tides.

11-20: Space Exploration and Technology

11. **SpaceX's Starship**: **SpaceX** is working on the **Starship**, a reusable spacecraft that could revolutionize space travel and pave the way for large-scale human exploration and colonization of other planets.
12. **Mars Colonization**: Companies like **SpaceX** and **Blue Origin** are investing in the conversion of Mars into a habitable space for humans, potentially solving Earth's population challenges.
13. **Asteroid Mining**: Companies like **Planetary Resources** and **Deep Space Industries** aim to mine asteroids for valuable resources like metals, water, and rare minerals.
14. **Solar Sails for Space Travel: The Planetary Society's LightSail project** is converting sunlight into propulsion, potentially enabling spacecraft to travel across vast distances in space with no fuel.
15. **Space Solar Power: Space-based solar panels** could beam solar energy from orbit down to Earth, avoiding weather-related interruptions and maximizing energy collection.
16. **Space Tourism**: Companies like **Blue Origin** and **Virgin Galactic** are making space tourism a reality, converting the dream of commercial space travel into an industry.
17. **Space Habitats: Bigelow Aerospace** is working on inflatable space habitats, which could one day convert space into living environments for astronauts, miners, and even tourists.
18. **Satellite Internet: Starlink**, a project by **SpaceX**, aims to create a global satellite internet system, converting satellite technology to provide fast internet to remote areas of Earth.
19. **Moon Bases**: Agencies like **NASA** and private companies are planning for lunar bases that could serve as stepping stones for

missions deeper into space, potentially converting the Moon into a site for resource extraction.

20. **Global Communication Networks**: The creation of global communication systems, like **Starlink**, could revolutionize internet access by converting satellite technology into a practical tool for global connectivity.

21-30: Economic and Financial Systems

21. **Cryptocurrency**: The rise of **Bitcoin, Ethereum**, and other cryptocurrencies is converting traditional banking systems into decentralized alternatives, enabling peer-to-peer transactions without the need for a centralized authority.

22. **Decentralized Finance (DeFi)**: **Uniswap** and other decentralized exchanges (DEXs) are turning traditional financial systems on their head by using blockchain technology to replace intermediaries in financial transactions.

23. **Digital Banking**: **Revolut** and **Monzo** are transforming banking by offering fully digital banking services, eliminating physical branches, and enabling users to manage their finances via smartphones.

24. **Blockchain for Supply Chain**: **IBM's Food Trust** blockchain is converting traditional supply chains into transparent, traceable networks, ensuring that products are ethically sourced and efficiently distributed.

25. **Artificial Intelligence in Finance**: **Betterment** and **Wealthfront** use AI to offer investment management, automating financial advice and trading to improve returns and reduce costs for consumers.

26. **Crowdfunding Platforms**: Platforms like **Kickstarter** and **Indiegogo** allow individuals to convert their ideas into reality

by collecting funds from a global pool of investors.

27. **Smart Contracts**: **Ethereum** and other blockchain platforms enable smart contracts, which automatically execute terms of an agreement without human intervention, reducing the need for third parties.

28. **Mobile Payment Systems**: **PayPal**, **Venmo**, and **Square** have converted traditional banking into easy-to-use mobile apps, allowing individuals to transfer money or make purchases quickly and securely from their smartphones.

29. **Peer-to-Peer Lending**: Platforms like **LendingClub** and **Prosper** are converting the traditional lending model into a decentralized one, allowing people to borrow and lend money directly to each other.

30. **Microloans**: Companies like **Kiva** are converting microloans into a tool for empowering entrepreneurs in developing countries, creating a more accessible global financial system.

31-40: Tech Innovation and Automation

31. **Robotics in Manufacturing**: **Boston Dynamics** and **ABB** are converting traditional manufacturing jobs into automated tasks, improving efficiency, and reducing human labor costs.

32. **Self-Driving Cars**: **Waymo** and **Tesla** are working on autonomous vehicles that could reduce traffic accidents and congestion, converting the transportation industry into one driven by AI and robotics.

33. **Smart Cities**: **Sidewalk Labs** (owned by Alphabet) is designing smart cities with intelligent infrastructure that optimizes everything from traffic flow to energy usage, converting urban environments into more efficient, sustainable spaces.

34. **3D Printing**: Companies like **Stratasys** and **Formlabs** are converting digital blueprints into physical objects, revolutionizing industries from healthcare (creating prosthetics) to construction (printing homes).
35. **Artificial Intelligence in Healthcare**: **IBM Watson Health** and **DeepMind** are developing AI that can analyze medical data, speeding up diagnoses and improving treatment outcomes, converting healthcare into a more efficient, data-driven field.
36. **Automation in Retail**: **Amazon** is using AI and robotics in warehouses to speed up product sorting and delivery, converting traditional logistics into a highly automated industry.
37. **Drone Delivery**: Companies like **Wing** (owned by Alphabet) are exploring the use of drones to convert delivery logistics into faster, more efficient services, particularly in remote areas.
38. **Virtual Reality (VR)**: **Oculus** and **HTC Vive** are converting entertainment and education into immersive virtual environments, where users can experience and interact with digital content in entirely new ways.
39. **Augmented Reality (AR)**: **Microsoft's HoloLens** and **Apple's ARKit** are converting the way people interact with the physical world by overlaying digital information on the real world, enhancing everything from gaming to retail.
40. **Voice Assistants**: **Amazon's Alexa, Google Assistant**, and **Apple's Siri** have converted voice commands into a primary interface for controlling devices, making interactions more intuitive and hands-free.

41-50: Agriculture and Sustainability

41. **Vertical Farming**: **AeroFarms** is pioneering vertical farming techniques that convert urban spaces into agricultural hubs, using minimal land and water to grow food efficiently in cities.

42. **Lab-Grown Meat**: **Memphis Meats** and **Impossible Foods** are working to convert traditional livestock farming into lab-grown alternatives that require fewer resources and create less environmental damage.

43. **Hydroponics**: **Freight Farms** has developed hydroponic farming units that convert shipping containers into fully functional farms, growing food in places with limited land and resources.

44. **Sustainable Packaging**: **Loop** is converting the traditional wasteful packaging system into a circular model where products are sold in reusable containers, reducing plastic waste.

45. **Electric Farming Equipment**: **John Deere** is developing electric tractors and farm equipment, converting fossil fuel-powered machinery into cleaner, more sustainable alternatives.

46. **Carbon Capture**: **Carbon Clean Solutions** and **Climeworks** are working on technologies that capture carbon from the atmosphere and convert it into useful products like fuel or building materials.

47. **Water Purification**: **Watergen** is developing technology that converts air humidity into clean drinking water, providing fresh water to areas with limited access to clean sources.

48. **Recycling Technology**: **TerraCycle** is pioneering recycling methods that convert hard-to-recycle waste into new products, reducing landfill waste and promoting a circular economy.

49. **Plastic-Eating Bacteria**: Scientists are experimenting with bacteria that convert plastic into biodegradable products,

potentially addressing the global plastic waste crisis.

50. **Sustainable Fishing**: **Wildtype** is creating lab-grown seafood, converting ocean resource extraction into sustainable farming methods that reduce the impact of overfishing.

These examples highlight a range of industries where **conversion**—from energy production to economic systems and environmental sustainability—is already happening, or is in development, creating a future where the vast resources of our planet and the universe are more efficiently utilized.

Unfortunately, there is not too much progress without profit

Chapter 3: Industry

Realistically, a modern economist is no stranger to industrialism. There will always be the need for factories. If you have a population then you need to provide products. So it's important to streamline the manufacturing process. We can do this by using artificial intelligence and automation to reduce production costs. These costs reductions will be offset by unemployment. However, this is a necessary investment to save much valuable time and money. In free markets, the price of competition will be constantly challenged. Supply and demand is the framework that keeps businesses and consumers in check. Basic logic tells us to buy a lower priced item whether or not it is made from machines. Socialistic economies put pressure on technological advancement because there is no incentive to invent and innovate. Privatization is about creating products that better suit the needs of the market. Competition creates diversity, which allows for better selection of products. More options the better. If we had 2 or 3 more aerospace companies that were just as competitive as Tesla, there would be a price reduction for space transport and travel. This means increased investment by the public. Staying afloat means researching and developing better, more efficient products. An alternate name for the space age is the space race. American competition with Russia and China is really the reason we put men on the moon and increased our aerospace budgets. No argument there, but we do need to mitigate the possibility of war as a result. This is dangerous, but history shows us that partnerships between the worlds superpowers is realistic and doable. We can avoid the Military-Industrial Complex. That's why it's called the International Space station. America was founded on a spirit of inquiry, so will be the next government/ organizing body in space. The problem with risky endeavors such as space travel is the insurance component. How do we deal with wrecks, malfunctions, and potential fatalities. Many people died in the discovery of the new world, but somehow European governments persevered and established colonies. When the challenger exploded in the 1980s, many people were critical of the increasing budgets. It took the wind out of our sails. We have problems here on earth why are we so worried about space. Why risk it. The reason why is because we increased standards of living, improved life span, and helped to prevent suffering. This is how progress works. No risk no reward. Bigger problems would never be solved without the courage and tenacity to advance in a more positive direction. Economics is also so important because the market is reactive and is based upon value. Markets allow for progress, but there needs to be sentimentality to glue together its inefficiencies. Building a factory may require local support. It may require an advertising campaign to convince people to seek employment. Industry especially, the space industry, needs to develop an economic culture. It needs to use economic principles with humanitarian goals as the foundation. Technological achievement is only possible with profit maximizing firms. Companies are sometimes more efficient than governments. People would benefit if Tesla lost some of its market share to competitors.

Industry, the concept of industrialization is explored as an essential foundation for modern economies, particularly when it comes to manufacturing, technological innovation, and space exploration. Below is a more detailed analysis of the ideas and examples provided in the paragraph, breaking down each point with in-depth explanation and relevant case studies.

1. Streamlining Manufacturing with Automation and AI

Industrial processes have historically been the backbone of economic growth. Automation, driven by **artificial intelligence (AI)**, has already begun transforming the manufacturing sector by improving efficiency, reducing production costs, and minimizing human error. These advancements are essential to maintain competitive advantage in a global market.

Examples:

- **Tesla's Gigafactories**: Tesla's use of automation in its Gigafactories is a prime example of how AI and robotics can streamline manufacturing. The company's advanced production lines significantly reduce labor costs while speeding up production times, leading to more affordable electric vehicles (EVs).
- **Fanuc Robotics**: This Japanese company is a leader in industrial automation, creating robotic systems that are integral to industries such as automotive manufacturing, electronics, and logistics. Their systems improve both quality control and speed, reducing operational costs.

By reducing labor costs through automation, manufacturers can scale production and lower prices for consumers, driving increased competition. While this could lead to some job displacement, the long-term economic benefit of reducing production costs and improving efficiency is undeniable.

2. Economic Impacts of Unemployment due to Automation

The rise of automation and artificial intelligence in manufacturing undoubtedly results in job displacement for many workers, particularly in manual labor-intensive industries. This shift creates a paradox where machines perform tasks traditionally done by humans, but it also opens new opportunities in sectors related to AI development, robotics, and advanced manufacturing techniques.

Examples:

- **Amazon Robotics**: Amazon's use of robots in warehouses has drastically reduced the need for human labor in certain tasks. However, this shift has led to the creation of jobs in engineering, robotics, software development, and warehouse management.
- **The Ford Motor Company's Moving Assembly Line**: Henry Ford revolutionized industrial manufacturing by introducing the moving assembly line, significantly reducing production costs. While this also displaced worker, it created a demand for factory supervisors, engineers, and specialists, ultimately stimulating job growth in other sectors.

Although unemployment can result from such advancements, economies that invest in re-skilling programs and education can mitigate the social impact by preparing workers for new opportunities in tech-driven industries in the future.

3. The Role of Free Markets and Competition

A central tenet of modern economics is the belief in free markets. The law of supply and demand serves as the foundation of how goods and services are produced, priced, and consumed. In the context of industrialism, competition leads to continuous innovation and the development of more diverse products. The key idea here is that competition forces companies to improve, innovate, and lower prices to meet the demand of consumers.

Examples:

- **Smartphone Industry**: Apple, Samsung, and Google are three major players in the smartphone market. Each company competes on various fronts, from price to technological innovation. This constant competition drives technological advancements (e.g., better camera quality, faster processors, and improved battery life) and keeps prices in check.
- **Aerospace Industry**: The development of space travel exemplifies how competition drives innovation. Companies like **SpaceX**, **Blue Origin**, and **Boeing** are competing to reduce the cost of space transportation. SpaceX's reusable rockets have drastically reduced the cost of launching payloads into space, revolutionizing the space industry and making space exploration more accessible.

The diversity resulting from competition benefits consumers by offering more choices and fostering an environment where quality and affordability coexist.

4. The Impact of Socialism on Technological Innovation

In socialistic economies, where resources and industries are often controlled by the government, there is typically less incentive for innovation due to the absence of profit-driven motives. This lack of competition can slow down technological advancements, as companies are not motivated to improve their products or services when profits are not the primary driver.

Examples:

- **Soviet Union's Space Program**: While the Soviet Union made significant strides in space exploration, including sending the first man into space (Yuri Gagarin), the government's centralized control led to inefficiencies. State-run initiatives lacked the competitive spirit of capitalist economies, which ultimately hindered rapid technological innovation in comparison to the private sector.
- **North Korea's Economy**: A current example of how a socialist economy can struggle with technological progress. Despite efforts in fields like space exploration, the lack of market competition and centralized planning has led to slower innovation in the country.

In contrast, market-driven economies like the U.S. and private companies such as **SpaceX** have continually pushed the boundaries of technology through the incentives of profitability and competition.

5. The Space Race: Government and Private Sector Collaboration

The space race of the mid-20th century, particularly between the U.S. and the Soviet Union, highlighted the importance of government funding in achieving technological milestones. However, this competition also brought about the involvement of private companies, further pushing innovation. While government agencies like **NASA** played a critical role in launching space missions, private companies are now becoming major players in the sector.

Examples:

- **NASA and SpaceX Partnership**: NASA and SpaceX exemplify public-private partnerships in space exploration. NASA provides funding and research, while SpaceX uses its private-sector efficiency and innovative capabilities to reduce launch costs and increase the frequency of missions.
- **Blue Origin**: Founded by Jeff Bezos, Blue Origin is competing with SpaceX to offer reusable rockets and affordable space tourism, demonstrating the ongoing importance of private sector investment in space technologies.

The collaboration between the public and private sectors can provide a balanced approach, where governmental regulation and funding combine with the efficiency and innovation of private companies to propel advancements in industries like aerospace.

6. Risk Management in High-Stakes Industries

High-risk industries, particularly space exploration, often face the challenge of risk management. The potential for disasters, such as the **Challenger disaster** in 1986, underscores the importance of developing robust insurance and safety protocols. As technologies advance, the inherent risks associated with space travel or industrial manufacturing also increase.

Examples:

- **SpaceX's Insurance Coverage**: SpaceX's innovative approach to reusing rockets significantly reduces the cost of space travel, but the company still faces substantial risk when launching missions. Insurance companies are essential in covering the risks of catastrophic failures, and SpaceX has worked closely with insurers to develop plans that mitigate these risks.

- **Aviation Industry's Safety Standards**: Companies like **Boeing** and **Airbus** invest heavily in developing and maintaining safety systems for airplanes, minimizing the risk of accidents. Despite the costs, ensuring safety remains a top priority, as demonstrated by the **737 MAX crisis** and the extensive safety measures Boeing implemented afterward.

In both space and manufacturing industries, careful risk management and insurance policies are essential to reduce the human, financial, and reputational impact of accidents. We want to make space travel less risky than driving a car.

7. Creating an Economic Culture within Industry

For industrial sectors to flourish, particularly new industries like space exploration, there must be a culture of innovation, competition, and collaboration. Competition can sometimes be ideological. This culture drives not only technological achievement but also economic growth. Industries should not merely be focused on profits but also consider humanitarian goals such as improving life expectancy, reducing poverty, and addressing global challenges.

Examples:

- **Tesla's Mission**: Tesla's goal is not only to create electric vehicles but also to combat climate change by accelerating the world's transition to sustainable energy. This mission has led to a unique economic culture where technological innovation serves a broader societal good.

- **Space Tourism**: **Virgin Galactic** and **Blue Origin** are creating an economic culture around space tourism, making space travel more accessible to the public and potentially expanding the tourism industry to new heights.

As companies develop a culture that blends economic growth with social responsibility, they contribute not only to industrial progress but also to positive global change.

8. Profit Maximization and Technological Achievement

Ultimately, the success of industrial ventures, particularly in high-stakes fields like space exploration, relies on the ability of companies to balance **profit maximization** with **technological achievement**. The key to achieving both is to continually innovate while ensuring that products are competitive, cost-effective, and meet the needs of consumers.

Examples:

- **Apple**: Apple's business model showcases how profitability can align with technological achievement. Its continuous innovation in products like the iPhone, iPad, and Apple Watch has made it one of the world's most profitable companies, all while leading the way in technology.
- **SpaceX**: By making reusable rockets, SpaceX not only maximizes its profits but also brings down the cost of space travel, paving the way for new industries like space tourism, satellite internet, and space colonization.

We discussed the integral role of industrialism in modern economies. As technological advances in automation, AI, and the space industry unfold, companies can reduce costs, foster innovation, and drive progress across various sectors. It's essential to maintain a competitive, profit-driven environment to ensure the continued development of technology while addressing global challenges like space exploration and sustainability.

Let's dive deeper into the points made in this chapter.

1. Streamlining Manufacturing with Automation and AI

BMW: The German carmaker uses automated robots to handle tasks like painting and assembling components, significantly improving production efficiency, and reducing human error.

Siemens: Siemens has incorporated AI-driven predictive maintenance solutions in their factories, ensuring equipment operates at optimal levels and reducing costly downtime.

Caterpillar: Using autonomous vehicles and mining equipment, Caterpillar has improved efficiency in mining operations while reducing the need for manual labor in hazardous environments.

Foxconn: The Taiwanese electronics manufacturer uses robotics and AI to assemble products like smartphones, especially at high-volume production sites, decreasing costs and increasing production rates.

Procter & Gamble: The company utilizes robotic systems to manage assembly lines, packaging, and logistics to improve throughput and reduce costs while ensuring product quality.

2. Economic Impact of Unemployment from Automation

Tesla's Gigafactories: While Tesla's factories use automation extensively, they also create specialized engineering, design, and software development jobs.

Amazon's Fulfillment Centers: Robotics have allowed Amazon to improve efficiency in warehouses, yet the company continues to hire thousands of human workers to manage AI and robotic systems.

Foxconn's Layoffs: The move to automation in Foxconn factories has led to reductions in assembly-line jobs, but increased demand for robotic engineers and systems developers.

Autonomous Vehicles (**Uber & Waymo**): Self-driving technology poses risks to truckers and delivery drivers but creates new opportunities for software developers and technicians specializing in autonomous systems.

General Motors: As GM automates more of its production line, some factory jobs are eliminated, but the company has created new positions in data analytics and automated manufacturing.

3. Role of Free Markets and Competition

Netflix vs. Blockbuster: Netflix revolutionized home entertainment through its digital streaming platform, driven by competition with Blockbuster. Netflix's success comes from its ability to provide customers with an innovative, convenient service.

Google vs. Yahoo: Google's competitive advantage was its innovative search algorithms, which made it the dominant search engine, while Yahoo struggled to innovate and diversify in the early 2000s.

Intel vs. AMD: Intel and AMD have fought a fierce competition for dominance in the semiconductor industry, with each company pushing the other to innovate continuously.

SpaceX vs. Boeing: Both companies are competing in the commercial space industry, with SpaceX leading in reusable rocket technology, while Boeing is focused on deep-space exploration systems.

Uber vs. Lyft: The competition between these two ridesharing giants has led to innovative developments such as autonomous ride-hailing, improved driver incentives, and expanding service coverage.

4. Impact of Socialism on Technological Innovation

Cuba's Biotechnology Sector: Cuba, with its centralized planning and limited market incentives, has made strides in biotechnology but has been slower than capitalist countries to scale innovations globally due to limited access to capital and technology.

North Korea's Military Industry: North Korea's state-run military industry has made advancements in missile technology, but the absence of competition has limited civilian applications and slowed broader technological innovation.

China's Government-Run Internet: Despite China's success in fostering companies like Huawei and Tencent, the government's tight control over the tech industry has stifled certain entrepreneurial endeavors in comparison to free-market counterparts like the U.S.

Soviet Space Program: While the Soviet Union achieved early milestones in space exploration, their centralized, state-run program lacked the flexibility and speed of private industry, limiting their overall space ambitions.

Venezuela's Oil Industry: The Venezuelan government's control over its oil industry has led to inefficiencies and corruption, stalling technological progress in oil extraction and refinement despite the country's vast oil reserves.

5. The Space Race: Government and Private Sector Collaboration

NASA & SpaceX: NASA's partnership with SpaceX has led to the development of the Falcon Heavy rocket, reducing the cost of sending astronauts and cargo to the International Space Station (ISS).

SpaceX & Boeing (Commercial Crew Program): NASA funded both SpaceX and Boeing to create private-sector spacecraft for transporting astronauts to the ISS. This partnership reduced NASA's reliance on Russian spacecraft.

NASA & Northrop Grumman: Northrop Grumman collaborated with NASA to develop the Cygnus spacecraft for resupply missions to the ISS, marking another example of public-private collaboration.

Blue Origin & NASA: Jeff Bezos' Blue Origin company worked with NASA to develop space habitats and technologies for moon missions, pushing for a sustainable human presence on the Moon.

ESA (European Space Agency) & Airbus: The ESA collaborates with Airbus to develop cutting-edge satellite technologies for Earth observation, weather forecasting, and communications.

6. Risk Management in High-Stakes Industries

Boeing's 737 MAX Insurance: After the tragic crashes of the 737 MAX, Boeing worked with insurance companies to mitigate risks and ensure passenger safety by upgrading its safety systems.

SpaceX's Falcon 9 Insurance: SpaceX uses comprehensive insurance policies for its rockets to cover launch failures, allowing the company to minimize the financial risks associated with space launches.

AIG and the Airline Industry: AIG provides extensive insurance coverage for airlines, helping manage risks related to crashes, natural disasters, and fleet maintenance, ensuring financial stability for airline companies.

Tesla's Autopilot Insurance: Tesla works with insurers to offer policies for vehicles equipped with autopilot technology, providing coverage in case of system malfunctions or accidents.

Nuclear Power Insurance: Nuclear power plants, due to the high-risk nature of their operations, work with specialized insurance providers like Lloyd's of London to cover potential catastrophes, accidents, and environmental damage.

7. Creating an Economic Culture within Industry

Tesla's Sustainability Mission: Tesla not only maximizes profits but also emphasizes sustainability, using renewable energy in its manufacturing processes and working toward a sustainable energy future.

Patagonia's Ethical Manufacturing: Patagonia's commitment to ethical manufacturing practices, such as using recycled materials and ensuring fair wages, has created a culture of environmental sustainability within the apparel industry.

Ben & Jerry's Social Responsibility: Ben & Jerry's focuses on social issues such as climate change, racial justice, and sustainable farming, building an economic culture rooted in humanitarian values.

Unilever's Sustainable Living Plan: Unilever promotes sustainability across its entire supply chain, from sourcing raw materials responsibly to improving environmental impact, setting an example for other companies.

The Body Shop's Fair Trade Movement: The Body Shop's commitment to fair trade and ethical sourcing has built a unique economic culture that appeals to socially conscious consumers.

8. Profit Maximization and Technological Achievement

Apple's iPhone Innovation: Apple's relentless focus on maximizing profits through the iPhone has driven it to innovate continuously, introducing new features like Face ID, OLED displays, and advanced processors, keeping the company at the forefront of the tech industry.

Google's Search Algorithm: Google uses its dominance in search to fund other technological innovations, such as AI, autonomous vehicles, and quantum computing, effectively using profit maximization to fund broader technological achievements.

Amazon's Web Services (AWS): Amazon Web Services is a profit-maximizing division of Amazon that funds its technological ventures, from cloud computing to AI development, revolutionizing industries worldwide.

Microsoft's Cloud Computing: Microsoft's Azure platform has allowed the company to compete with Amazon and Google, making massive profits while simultaneously advancing cloud technologies.

Microsoft's Acquisition of LinkedIn: Microsoft's acquisition of LinkedIn allowed it to integrate AI and data analytics into its productivity tools, further enhancing the company's technological edge and profit margins.

Conclusion

The examples above show the tangible benefits and challenges of implementing the principles we just discussed, such as the need for free-market competition, the integration of automation, and collaboration between the public and private sectors. By analyzing these examples, it's clear that while automation and technological advancements offer significant economic benefits, they must be balanced with risk management, a competitive market environment, and a culture that prioritizes innovation, social responsibility, and sustainability. Through the ongoing evolution of industries, particularly in space, manufacturing, and technology, these principles continue to shape the modern economy.

Chapter 4: Real Estate

A modern economy is essentially a space-faring civilization. Modern economics means solving spatial distancing. People take up space and therefore it's crucial to acquire more of it. Land rights and ownership should exist in space dwellings as well. Developing habitats out of this planet is crucial for future human life outside of earth. Rent must be as cheap as possible and of course safe. When settlers built homes in North America there were many problems with resources and safety. We need to finance something sustainable. It's one thing to go into space but another thing to stay and live there. You and I both know this is an incredibly expensive project to undertake. Right now given the current state of human affairs and technology, the costs outweigh the benefits. But in the future this will be important to deal with overpopulation. Crowded cities on earth deal with sanitation and public health issues. Food, water, and transportation needs to be efficient and not that costly. Expanding to other areas of the solar system and in orbit around earth is critical to developing a modern economic system. Communication with the ground is important, but there also needs to be businesses providing space networks. This means slowly allowing private businesses to open shop in space. If there are no public and private companies then all endeavors would be by governments. Bureaucracy in space is a slow and painful process because there are no incentives to innovate and spread wealth. Some businesses are even more efficient than the government. They organize people better. Space ex is taking that leap by planning to colonize mars. There may not be a charter to do so, although they may get some help from the government. We do have space-force for security purposes thanks to the American government. So where is the land and what type of land is it? Mars is mostly desolate. A desert of rocks, valleys, cliffs, and expanses. If we can somehow mine the ice sheets under the Martian surface, we would be one step closer to sustainability. We can use weapons of mass destruction to clear land and alter the geography. Terraforming a planet is not an easy process but it's a brilliant task to undertake. Altering the landscape to better suit the needs of human civilizations is a good goal. In the early days of the new world mercantilism allowed European countries to build a trading network between three continents. If planets like mars had useable land (chemicals, minerals, raw materials, and resources.) then it makes sense to mine that and make money doing it. Remember economics is about land, labor, and resources.

In-Depth Analysis of Chapter 4: Real Estate in Space

Chapter 4 explores the expanding frontier of space colonization and the potential for real estate to become a key factor in the future of human civilization. The chapter touches on themes of scarcity, property rights, land acquisition, and how economic systems can be adapted to outer space. While today's economic systems are rooted in the land-based, resource-driven dynamics of Earth, the push into space requires a rethinking of these principles in an environment where resources are limited, and technological solutions are not yet mature. The future of real estate, particularly in space, offers a set of unique challenges and opportunities.

At its core, space-faring civilization hinges on solving the problem of "special distancing"—the spatial constraints of living on Earth. As Earth's population grows and resources become more constrained, the concept of acquiring space—both physical land and new economic territories—becomes increasingly important. Real estate on other planets, particularly Mars, as well as in orbital stations, could serve as a solution to problems like overcrowding, resource depletion, and environmental degradation on Earth.

This chapter suggests that land rights and ownership in space are not just theoretical; they will become essential as humanity ventures off Earth and into the cosmos. In many ways, these ideas are similar to the early days of European colonialism, where settlers faced challenges of resource scarcity, safety, and economic sustainability in newly discovered territories. Just as it was difficult to establish colonies in the New World, the challenges facing space colonization will be no less complex.

Key themes in this analysis involve:

1. **Land rights and ownership**: How will property rights be structured in space? Who will own the land, and who will manage its use?
2. **Development of sustainable habitats**: How can we build long-term, habitable environments on other planets, such as Mars?
3. **Private sector participation**: The balance between government agencies and private businesses in space colonization.
4. **Terraforming and resource extraction**: The process of altering a planet's environment and extracting resources to make space habitable.
5. **Mercantilism and trade networks**: The idea of developing economic systems in space, much like the mercantile systems that formed during the early age of exploration.

Now, let's examine 50 specific examples that elaborate on these points, particularly focusing on industries, companies, and technologies that can play crucial roles in space real estate development and space-faring economies.

50 Examples to Elaborate on Space Real Estate

1. Land Rights & Ownership in Space

1. **Lunar Property Rights (Private Companies)**: Companies like **LunarX** and **Moon Express** are exploring the idea of land ownership on the Moon, aiming to establish lunar mining colonies.
2. **International Treaties (Outer Space Treaty)**: The **1967 Outer Space Treaty** limits claims of sovereignty over celestial bodies, but future treaties may establish new frameworks for land ownership and development.
3. **Mars One Project**: The **Mars One** mission's plan to send settlers to Mars involves private ownership of the land, sparking debates about the legal right to claim extraterrestrial territory.
4. **Asteroid Mining Companies (Planetary Resources)**: **Planetary Resources**, a company focused on mining asteroids for precious metals, is exploring ownership of mined resources from space bodies.
5. **Moon Village (ESA)**: The **European Space Agency** envisions a **Moon Village** in which various nations and private entities own and develop lunar land for resource extraction and habitation.

2. Sustainable Habitats in Space

6. **SpaceX's Starship**: **SpaceX's Starship** is designed to be a fully reusable spacecraft that will play a critical role in transporting settlers to Mars, providing the foundation for future space communities.

7. **NASA's Artemis Program**: NASA's **Artemis Program** will establish a sustainable lunar base, setting the groundwork for developing habitats beyond Earth.

8. **Bigelow Aerospace**: **Bigelow Aerospace** is working on inflatable habitats designed for use in low Earth orbit or on other celestial bodies.

9. **The O'Neill Cylinder (NASA/Private Ventures)**: The concept of an **O'Neill Cylinder**—large rotating space habitats—aims to create self-sustaining environments in space.

10. **Lunar Base Alpha (NASA)**: The planned **Lunar Base Alpha** would be the first permanent human habitat on the Moon, offering insight into how we might build long-term habitats on other planets.

---

3. Private Sector Involvement in Space Colonization

11. **Blue Origin**: **Blue Origin**, founded by Jeff Bezos, aims to establish a human presence in space through reusable rockets and the development of space habitats in low Earth orbit (LEO).

12. **Virgin Galactic**: **Virgin Galactic**, led by Richard Branson, is positioning itself as a leader in commercial space tourism, laying the groundwork for private sector involvement in space.

13. **Lockheed Martin**: **Lockheed Martin**'s collaboration with NASA on the **Orion spacecraft** is pivotal in preparing for space exploration and colonization.
14. **Sierra Nevada Corporation (Dream Chaser)**: **Dream Chaser**, a reusable spacecraft by **Sierra Nevada Corporation**, is being developed for resupply missions to the ISS and future space colonies.
15. **SpaceX's Starlink**: The **Starlink** satellite network, designed by SpaceX, could form the backbone of future communication infrastructure for space settlements.

4. Terraforming & Resource Extraction

16. **Terraforming Mars (NASA and SpaceX)**: NASA's studies of **Martian terraforming** could potentially make Mars more habitable for humans by altering its atmosphere and temperature.
17. **Mars Ice Mining (ESA)**: **ESA** is exploring methods to mine the **ice** on Mars, which could provide essential water for human settlers.
18. **Mining Asteroids (Deep Space Industries)**: **Deep Space Industries** is looking into asteroid mining to extract valuable resources like water, platinum, and iron.
19. **Helium-3 Mining (Moon Express)**: **Moon Express** is researching the feasibility of mining **Helium-3** from the Moon for use in future fusion energy production.
20. **Lunar Helium-3 (China's Chang'e Program)**: China's **Chang'e program** is advancing efforts to explore and mine lunar resources, particularly Helium-3.

5. Mercantilism and Space Economy

21. **Space-based Solar Power (Japan)**: **Japan's** efforts to develop space-based solar power would generate energy in space and transmit it to Earth, potentially powering lunar, or Martian colonies.
22. **Space Tourism (Blue Origin and Virgin Galactic)**: The development of **space tourism** through companies like **Virgin Galactic** and **Blue Origin** is expanding the space economy and paving the way for private space ventures.
23. **Asteroid Resource Trade (Planetary Resources)**: Companies like **Planetary Resources** are positioning themselves to create space-based trading networks for minerals and rare metals.
24. **Mars Colonization (Elon Musk's Vision)**: **Elon Musk's** vision for **SpaceX** includes creating self-sustaining colonies on Mars, potentially driving a new economy focused on resource extraction, agriculture, and tourism.
25. **Private Space Stations (Axiom Space)**: **Axiom Space** plans to build commercial space stations, contributing to the emerging economy of space-based commerce and habitation.

---

6. Economic Sustainability and Cost Challenges

26. **Recycling in Space (NASA's Sustainability Goals)**: NASA's efforts to develop recycling systems for water, air, and waste will make long-term space habitation more economically viable.
27. **In-Situ Resource Utilization (ISRU)**: The use of **ISRU** on Mars to extract water, oxygen, and fuel from the local environment

reduces the costs of bringing supplies from Earth.

28. **Space Mining (AstroScale)**: **AstroScale** is working to remove space debris, thus ensuring safer, cheaper access to space, and supporting future commercial activities in low Earth orbit.
29. **SpaceX's Cost-Reduction Goals**: SpaceX's development of reusable rockets significantly reduces the cost of launching cargo and settlers into space.
30. **Lunar Greenhouses (NASA's LUNA Project)**: NASA's **LUNA** project aims to develop self-sustaining agricultural systems for use on the Moon, making space colonies more self-reliant and cost-efficient.

7. Space Security and Governance

31. **Space Force (U.S. Military)**: The creation of **Space Force** ensures the security of satellite infrastructure and space-based assets critical to the growing space economy.
32. **UN's Outer Space Governance**: The **United Nations** is working on frameworks to establish **international laws** governing space resources, property rights, and territorial claims.
33. **Space Traffic Management (Space Surveillance Network)**: The **Space Surveillance Network** tracks objects in space to prevent collisions and maintain order as the space economy grows.
34. **Cybersecurity for Space Assets (NASA and Private Companies)**: Protecting space-based infrastructure from cyber-attacks will be critical to maintaining the stability of the space economy.
35. **Lunar Resource Allocation (International Agreements)**: International agreements may

be required to manage and fairly allocate
resources extracted from the Moon, ensuring
peace and collaboration between spacefaring
nations.

8. Interplanetary Trade and Expansion

36. **Spaceports (Spaceport America)**:
Spaceport America is an operational hub
for private spacecraft, with potential to
become a key point of entry for goods and
services from space to Earth.
37. **Interplanetary Cargo Delivery (SpaceX's
Starship)**: **SpaceX's Starship** could be
used to carry goods between Earth, the
Moon, and Mars, facilitating interplanetary
trade.
38. **Lunar Base Operations (NASA)**: NASA's
planned lunar base would support
commercial ventures and mining operations,
creating a bustling economy in space.
39. **Martian Commerce (SpaceX and Blue
Origin)**: Future Martian settlements would
create a need for commercial hubs to
support trade between Earth and Mars.
40. **Satellite Internet (OneWeb)**: **OneWeb** is
developing satellite internet technology that
will be used in space and on Earth, creating
an essential communication network for
interplanetary commerce.

9. Long-term Space Exploration and Colonization

41. **Terraforming Mars (SpaceX's Starship)**:
The idea of **terraforming** Mars into a more
Earth-like environment is being researched
by various groups, including **SpaceX**.

42. **Permanent Lunar Base (NASA and Private Companies)**: Private companies partnering with **NASA** to establish a permanent base on the Moon will contribute to the expansion of space as a habitable zone.

43. **Space Mining (Deep Space Industries)**: **Deep Space Industries** is focused on mining asteroids and bringing valuable minerals back to Earth or future space colonies.

44. **Autonomous Lunar Agriculture (SpaceX)**: **SpaceX** aims to develop autonomous agricultural systems for the Moon that will be crucial for sustaining life in space.

45. **Mars Habitat Development (Blue Origin)**: **Blue Origin**'s focus on developing the infrastructure needed to establish human colonies on Mars involves building habitats that can withstand the harsh conditions on the planet.

---

10. Bridging the Gap Between Earth and Space

46. **Space-Based Solar Power (Japan)**: **Japan** is pursuing the development of **space-based solar power** to generate energy that can be transmitted back to Earth, thus ensuring sustainable energy supplies for space colonies.

47. **Lunar Mining (China's Chang'e Program)**: China's efforts to mine the Moon's resources will pave the way for interplanetary trade and provide the resources needed for future space development.

48. **Orbital Manufacturing (Made In Space)**: **Made In Space** is working on **3D printing** in microgravity environments, which could

lead to the production of goods in orbit to supply future space stations.

49. **Space Tourism (Virgin Galactic)**: **Virgin Galactic** and other companies' push into **space tourism** will lead to a burgeoning market for private space ventures.

50. **Interplanetary Communications (SpaceX and Starlink)**: The development of **Starlink** satellite networks could allow for high-speed communication across the solar system, enabling the smooth operation of businesses and governments in space.

This detailed analysis illustrates how **space real estate** is more than just a futuristic concept; it's an evolving industry with tangible steps being taken today to make the dream of human civilization beyond Earth a reality. The future of real estate in space will hinge on legal frameworks, resource extraction, sustainable living, and the cooperation of private and public entities.

Chapter 5: Meritocracy

When your personal skill set becomes social it makes sense to reward based upon tangible results. A modern economy needs to be practical so that we incentivize good economic behavior. Welfare systems fail to support economic progress. We want people to make goals and gain a sense of accomplishment after achieving them. This is important in investing, because it lets stock holders know that they will get a return on investment. Realistically, not everything will be on merit, but if we allow employers to gain higher security clearance in the space race based upon economic results, we can positively influence human progress. Space is really a reward for good work. It truly is the final frontier, but, we need the financing to get there. Space is a backdrop for a greater social order. People need something to look forward to a sense of excitement and adventure. If we want to alleviate the masses from the emotional debt of being a human then we need a bright future to fix our problems. We need to be futuristic. We need to encourage younger generations to pay it forward. Space can help piggyback an increase in the standard of living by providing a theatre of economic and technological operations.

In Chapter 5, the discussion about meritocracy and its relation to space exploration and economic systems touches on some interesting and complex ideas. Let's break down and elaborate on these key concepts:

1. **Meritocracy and Equal Initial Endowment**: The argument here is that if everyone had equal resources and opportunities from the start, we could

theoretically create a meritocratic system where people are rewarded solely based on their abilities, skills, and accomplishments. Meritocracy hinges on the belief that success should be earned, not given—this incentivizes individuals to work hard and be productive, which is good for the economy.

2. **Meritocracy as a Tool for Social and Economic Progress**: The idea is that a meritocratic system encourages individuals to pursue excellence and tangible results. In a modern economy, this would mean rewarding people or companies that achieve economic success or contribute to technological advancements. This creates a system where effort is directly linked to outcomes, and people can see that working hard will lead to tangible rewards—whether in terms of income, recognition, or career advancement.

3. **Economic Incentives and Welfare Systems**: Welfare systems often aim to support people who are struggling, but the argument here is that welfare may not do enough to drive long-term economic growth or progress. By incentivizing individuals to pursue their goals through hard work and achievement (in a meritocratic system), economic behavior can be more aligned with growth. The idea is that people should have goals that are ambitious and rewarding, both for themselves and society. Welfare might provide temporary relief, but it could also reduce incentives for people to strive toward higher achievement.

4. **Space Exploration as a Reward for Good Work**: The link between meritocracy and space exploration is that space could serve as a reward for society's best work. Since space exploration is a monumental challenge and requires a high level of technical, economic, and social achievement, the argument is that space programs could be a way to motivate and reward the collective effort of people and nations. By encouraging people to strive for excellence, space exploration becomes a symbol of humanity's ability to solve complex problems and work together toward a grand goal.

5. **Space as the Final Frontier and a Bright Future**: Space is seen here as a representation of the "next step" for human progress, a challenge that requires significant innovation and resourcefulness. By framing space exploration as something to look forward to, there is a sense of optimism and excitement about the future. The idea is that if people have something extraordinary to aim for, such as space exploration, it can drive progress across many sectors of society—technologically, economically, and socially.

6. **The Role of Younger Generations**: Encouraging younger generations to "pay it forward" connects the concept of meritocracy with a forward-looking, generational perspective. If the current generation invests in scientific, technological, and economic advancements, future generations will benefit and be able to build upon those successes. Space, in this

context, can be a powerful motivator for young people, inspiring them to work hard and aim for high achievements that will benefit humanity as a whole.

7.   **Space and Standard of Living**: The idea of space exploration as a "theatre of economic and technological operations" suggests that, while the pursuit of space is a lofty goal, it can have practical benefits for everyday life. As we develop technologies for space exploration, these innovations often find applications in other areas of society, which can raise the standard of living. For example, advancements in materials science, telecommunications, and robotics that come from space programs often end up benefiting various sectors of the economy, from medicine to manufacturing.

In essence, the chapter discusses how a meritocratic system, while not perfect, could incentivize economic and social progress, with space exploration serving as a grand and practical goal that both motivates people and drives technological development. The idea is that meritocracy, if applied effectively, can create a system where people are rewarded for their skills and contributions, ultimately leading to a better future for everyone.

Chapter 6: Universal Currency

In a future where space exploration, technological innovation, and economic systems are intertwined, a Universal Currency (UC) could be the cornerstone for this ambitious vision. This currency would need to serve as a global, digital asset, accessible, and usable across borders, transcending geographical, economic, and political boundaries. Here's an outline for designing a Universal Currency that aligns with the principles of this modern economic framework:

1. Digital and Inclusive Design

The Universal Currency would be fully digital, operating on a decentralized blockchain network that ensures transparency, security, and inclusivity. It would be universally accessible through devices like smartphones, tablets, or even directly integrated into communication systems, enabling anyone—regardless of location or financial status—to participate in the global economy. This would remove barriers to financial inclusion and break down geographical constraints, as citizens of developing nations could seamlessly access economic opportunities on the same platform as those in developed nations.

2. Backed by a Resource-Intelligent System

Rather than relying solely on gold, precious metals, or fiat-backed systems, the Universal Currency would be backed by a "Resource Basket" that integrates multiple assets. These assets would include space-based resources, sustainable energy sources (e.g., solar power, nuclear fusion), and critical technologies like AI, automation, and robotics. Space mining, lunar or asteroid mining, and energy derived from nuclear fission and fusion would contribute to a resource pool that stabilizes the currency's value and creates an innovative form of resource-backed money. This future-focused system would evolve as new technologies and space resources emerge.

3. AI-Driven Economic Decision Making

AI and smart contracts would be embedded within the currency's ecosystem, allowing for automatic economic decision-making that can dynamically adjust to global needs. This could include adjusting interest rates, managing supply and demand, and optimizing trade routes or financial flows. The AI system would help to reduce inefficiencies in credit, lending, and trade by ensuring that resources are distributed to areas of highest need and greatest potential. By doing so, it would prevent market instability and help create a more resilient and efficient global economy.

4. Sustainability and Equity

The currency system would be inherently linked to sustainability goals. A portion of transactions would automatically contribute to projects aimed at solving energy and food crises, space exploration, and the development of new technologies that support long-term ecological balance. Additionally, the currency could implement an equity-based model, rewarding individuals, companies, and nations for environmentally responsible practices, energy efficiency, and sustainable resource management. The goal would be to ensure the health of both Earth and space economies, creating value from collaboration and responsible resource use.

5. Interplanetary Financial System

The Universal Currency must be able to function across both Earth and space. As humanity advances into space, the currency would be crucial for interplanetary trade and commerce, including the development of industries like space mining, tourism, and energy production from celestial bodies. This would also necessitate the creation of interplanetary banking systems, allowing for real-time transactions between Earth and space colonies (such as on Mars or in the International Space Station). The currency would facilitate resource sharing, investments in space infrastructure, and economic growth in previously uncharted territories.

6. Decentralized Governance

The Universal Currency would be governed by a decentralized global coalition of governments, international organizations, and private enterprises, ensuring that no single entity has sole control over the currency. This decentralized governance model would enable broader participation, transparency, and democratic decision-making processes, in line with the principles of democracy and global cooperation. This structure would also be crucial in navigating political resistance and ensuring that the currency's implementation benefits humanity equitably.

7. Meritocracy and Innovation

A key component of the Universal Currency is its alignment with the meritocratic values of modern economics. The currency system could reward innovation, creativity, and achievement. Individuals and organizations contributing to scientific progress, such as breakthroughs in space exploration, energy, healthcare, or AI, would receive financial incentives that fuel further research and development. Similarly, countries or corporations that excel in space infrastructure or technological advancements would gain economic benefits, promoting a competitive spirit similar to the "space race" metaphor, but rooted in collaborative progress.

8. Global and Local Stability

The currency would be designed to stabilize economic systems both globally and locally. It could be programmed with features that automatically adjust based on global financial trends or crises, reducing volatility. However, it would also allow local economies to operate autonomously by providing custom economic tools and mechanisms specific to each region's needs. This would ensure that while the currency functions globally, local economic structures can thrive without the risks of overwhelming external interference or instability.

9. Security, Privacy, and Ethical Standards

Security would be paramount in a Universal Currency. Built on advanced encryption and blockchain technology, the system would safeguard users' assets and personal data. Ethical standards would guide the use of AI and data analytics within the currency framework, ensuring that privacy is maintained and that individuals retain control over their economic decisions. At the same time, the system would allow for anti-fraud and anti-money laundering measures to ensure the integrity of the global economy.

10. Education and Public Awareness

To ensure that people across the world understand and trust the Universal Currency, widespread education and outreach would be essential. International educational programs would focus on digital literacy, economic systems, space exploration, and the benefits of a shared global currency. By engaging the public in a grassroots movement—through media, music, and education—the Universal Currency could be integrated into daily life as an empowering tool for global progress.

In summary, the Universal Currency would be an adaptive, decentralized digital currency designed to integrate the principles of sustainability, space exploration, technological advancement, and global cooperation. Its implementation would empower individuals and governments alike, fostering a meritocratic society that rewards innovation and progress. With careful planning, international collaboration, and a commitment to equity, the Universal Currency could become the backbone of a new economic era that is inclusive, efficient, and space-bound.

II. Microeconomics: Individual and Firm-Level Impact

At the microeconomic level, the Universal Currency would have a profound effect on the way individuals and firms interact with the economy. Let's apply some key microeconomic concepts to see how it might work:

1. Supply and Demand

In microeconomics, **supply and demand** dictate the price and availability of goods and services. With the Universal Currency, supply and demand dynamics could be influenced in innovative ways:

- **Supply** of resources would be expanded through the utilization of space-based resources like asteroid mining, solar power from space, or lunar minerals. This dramatically increases the supply of raw materials and energy, decreasing scarcity.

- **Demand** would be influenced by global population growth, technological advancements, and the need for sustainable resources. As space exploration and colonization create new frontiers for resource acquisition, demand would shift from Earth-bound resources to those harvested from space, altering pricing mechanisms globally.

In a competitive market for space resources or space technologies, **prices** for space exploration and energy could fluctuate based on demand from Earth and space colonies, while supply-side advancements—such as better space transportation—could lower costs.

2. Incentives and Market Behavior

The Universal Currency, backed by space resources and AI-driven systems, would change the incentives for individuals and firms:

- **Merit-based rewards**: Firms or individuals contributing to advancements in space exploration, energy production, or AI-driven technologies would be incentivized financially. In economics, **incentives** drive behavior, and the currency system would reward those who generate innovations.

- **Market structure**: The introduction of space-based industries could create **monopolistic competition** or **oligopolies** in emerging sectors, such as space mining or AI automation. Firms in these sectors may compete to innovate and dominate markets, and the **barriers to entry** could be influenced by the cost of technology, research, and development.

3. Resource Allocation

In microeconomics, one of the central ideas is how resources are **allocated**. The UC system, being backed by space resources, would encourage **efficient resource allocation** across both Earth and space. Artificial intelligence embedded within the currency would optimize resource allocation based on real-time economic needs. For example:

- Space-based mining companies could optimize their resource extraction strategies, directing efforts where the most valuable resources are found (such as minerals on asteroids).

- AI systems could guide firms in Earth's markets, ensuring that resources (whether labor, capital, or raw materials) are allocated to the most productive sectors.

4. Externalities

The concept of **externalities**—both positive and negative—applies here. For instance:

- **Positive externalities**: Technological advancements in space, such as AI or renewable energy breakthroughs, would spill over into Earth-bound industries, boosting productivity and efficiency in sectors like healthcare or manufacturing.

- **Negative externalities**: Space exploration or resource extraction from other planets could create environmental risks, such as space debris. Addressing these externalities through regulation or incentives would be important to ensure that the long-term effects of space activities don't harm humanity or the environment.

III. Macroeconomics: Broader Economic Implications

At the macroeconomic level, the Universal Currency would deeply impact global trade, monetary policy, and economic growth. Let's explore some key macroeconomic principles and how they relate to the UC system:

1. Monetary Policy

The creation of a global, digital Universal Currency would lead to **global monetary policy** shifts. Traditionally, central banks control currency supply and interest rates to stabilize economies. In the UC framework:

- **Central banks** or **global economic bodies** would likely oversee the regulation of the currency. They would have the responsibility to **manage inflation** and **maintain stable prices**, but AI systems might assist in adjusting interest rates or the supply of currency based on global economic conditions.

- The UC's **value stability** would be derived not just from Earth-based reserves but from **space assets**, ensuring that it doesn't fluctuate wildly like traditional currencies. This stability could reduce economic volatility.

2. International Trade and Globalization

The Universal Currency would drive **global trade** by facilitating transactions across borders, eliminating the complexity of foreign exchange markets. In macroeconomics, this is called **global economic integration**. With space exploration as the new frontier for trade:

- **Interplanetary trade**: We could see the emergence of trade between Earth and space colonies, creating new sectors of trade in space tourism, research, and resource exchange. The Universal Currency would serve as the medium for such exchanges.

- **Efficiency in trade**: The currency's AI-driven system could optimize global supply chains, reducing **transaction costs** and **information asymmetries**. This would make trade more efficient, ensuring that goods and services flow smoothly across the globe.

3. Economic Growth and Investment

The Universal Currency could act as a catalyst for **economic growth**, both on Earth and in space. By incentivizing technological development, space exploration, and the expansion of sustainable energy sources:

- **Capital investment**: The UC would encourage investment in new technologies by making it easier to access financing globally. This could lead to rapid advancements in industries like robotics, energy production, and healthcare.

- **Long-term growth**: By promoting space exploration and the efficient use of resources, we could unlock a new phase of **economic expansion** where the **global GDP** is no longer constrained by Earth's finite resources. The growth of space colonies could lead to new industries and new wealth, driving long-term macroeconomic prosperity.

4. Global Inequality and Equity

A critical macroeconomic concern is the reduction of **global inequality**. The Universal Currency would play a role in making economic opportunities accessible to all, regardless of geography:

- **Financial inclusion**: By removing barriers to entry in global markets, the UC would allow underserved populations to access economic opportunities previously unavailable to them, thus reducing income inequality.

- **Resource redistribution**: The UC system could also incorporate mechanisms to redistribute wealth from the rich (who benefit from space-based resources) to the poor, ensuring that the benefits of technological and space exploration advancements are shared equitably.

5. Employment and Labor Markets

The introduction of automation, AI, and space technologies would transform the **labor market**. **Microeconomics** focuses on individual firms and workers, while **macroeconomics** considers broader employment trends:

- **Labor displacement**: As automation replaces manual labor, there could be job losses in traditional sectors. However, the creation of new industries (e.g., space travel, AI innovation) would offset this displacement, although retraining and education will be critical.

- **Universal Basic Income (UBI)**: The concept of UBI, discussed in the context of the UC, could provide an economic cushion to those displaced by technological advancements, promoting **economic stability** and reducing social unrest.

IV. Conclusion: Integrating Micro and Macro in the Universal Currency System

In conclusion, the **Universal Currency** represents a holistic economic system that applies both **microeconomic** and **macroeconomic** principles to create a sustainable, technologically advanced, and inclusive global economy. By merging concepts like **supply and demand, resource allocation, monetary policy, global trade,** and **economic growth**, it sets the stage for a future where technology, space exploration, and sustainable resource use drive the global economy.

While this vision is ambitious, it offers a compelling example of how economic systems might evolve to meet the challenges of a rapidly changing world. The success of such a system would depend on careful planning, international collaboration, and the application of core economic principles to balance innovation, equity, and sustainability.

I. The Nature of the Universal Currency (UC)

The **Universal Currency (UC)** aims to integrate diverse economic systems—Earth-bound and space-faring—by creating a global digital currency, designed to be efficient, secure, and universally accessible. It is backed not by traditional fiat money or precious metals but by **space resources**, **sustainable technologies**, and **AI-driven economic systems**. This represents a profound shift from traditional monetary policy frameworks. Space materials can be like the gold standard of Universal Currency. Just to add, nnother term for UC would be "Space Bucks."

II. Microeconomic Implications

A. Resource Allocation and Efficiency

In a traditional economy, resources are allocated based on **supply and demand**, and pricing mechanisms adjust accordingly. However, in a system backed by space resources and AI, we encounter an additional layer of complexity. The presence of **space-based resources**—such as asteroid mining, solar energy from space, and lunar minerals—introduces a **new frontier** for resource allocation.

- **Resource Scarcity**: Earth's scarcity of critical raw materials (such as rare earth metals) could be alleviated by mining resources from celestial bodies. This would drastically lower input costs for industries reliant on these materials, such as electronics, renewable energy, and space infrastructure. Consequently, this could reduce **prices** for certain technologies and increase the **supply** of high-tech goods, thereby boosting **consumer welfare**.

- **Technological Externalities**: As new technologies (e.g., AI, space exploration, nuclear fusion) emerge, they produce **positive externalities**—benefits that spill over to other sectors. For instance, advances in space technology could lead to innovations in robotics, materials science, and even healthcare, creating a **virtuous cycle of innovation**. The **spillover effect** could foster cross-sectoral productivity growth and technological diffusion.

- **AI-Driven Economic Decisions**: The **AI systems** integrated into the UC could improve the efficiency of resource distribution by minimizing **transaction costs** and **coordination failures**. AI could streamline supply chains, improve production scheduling, and better forecast future resource needs. This would lower the **cost of capital**, as firms could be more confident in future economic conditions.

B. Market Structure and Competition

The introduction of space-based industries would create new **market structures**. New sectors such as **space tourism, space mining**, and **space construction** could either evolve into monopolistic markets or more competitive ones, depending on barriers to entry:

- **Monopolistic Competition**: Space industries could initially be dominated by a small number of firms with significant access to space-based resources and technologies. However, once these technologies become more widespread, **monopolistic competition** might emerge, where firms differentiate themselves based on quality, price, or innovation. The competitive pressures would encourage firms to innovate continuously, especially as **space exploration becomes more feasible**.

- **Innovation Incentives**: Under the Universal Currency system, the reward for innovation could be integrated directly into the currency system. Individuals, firms, and nations that contribute to space exploration or other technological advances would receive **direct economic rewards**, motivating continued innovation. For example, if a company develops a cheaper method for space mining, the resulting **reduction in input costs** could significantly lower the cost of other technologies on Earth, benefitting consumers globally.

C. Consumer Behavior and Financial Inclusion

The Universal Currency's **digital nature** makes it a powerful tool for **financial inclusion**. Individuals who were previously excluded from traditional financial systems—due to geographical location, financial literacy, or political instability—would gain access to the global economy.

- **Consumer Decision-Making**: With the UC, consumers would be empowered by the ability to make transactions seamlessly across borders, without dealing with exchange rate fluctuations or regional financial restrictions. The UC would also enable **smarter consumption decisions** by providing real-time data about supply and demand trends, ensuring that consumers have the necessary information to make **informed purchasing decisions**.

- **Behavioral Economics**: The UC could be designed to include mechanisms that promote **sustainable consumer behavior**. For example, consumers could be incentivized to choose products that are **environmentally friendly** or **energy-efficient** by receiving rewards or discounts in the UC system. This aligns with principles of **nudging** in behavioral economics, where small incentives are used to promote socially beneficial outcomes.

III. Macroeconomic Implications

A. Global Trade and Economic Integration

At the macroeconomic level, the UC has the potential to revolutionize **global trade** and economic integration. In traditional systems, international trade is impeded by **exchange rates**, **transaction costs**, and **trade barriers** (e.g., tariffs, quotas). The UC, operating as a **universal digital currency**, removes many of these obstacles.

- **Currency Efficiency**: As a **single global currency**, the UC would eliminate the need for multiple currencies and complex **foreign exchange mechanisms**, significantly reducing **currency risk** and **transaction costs** in global trade. This could boost cross-border investment flows and make **global supply chains** more efficient.

- **Interplanetary Trade**: As space exploration and colonization expand, the **Universal Currency** would be used for trade between Earth and space colonies. This would introduce a new set of goods and services, such as **space minerals, energy sources from space**, or **space tourism**. The UC would make these transactions frictionless, unlocking entirely new economic opportunities and industries.

- **Balance of Trade**: The ability to access space-based resources could shift global trade balances. Nations or corporations with access to lucrative space resources could potentially become **net exporters** of raw materials, while Earth-bound nations could specialize in **high-tech manufacturing** or **service industries**.

B. Economic Growth and Technological Progress

A major driver of the UC system is the promotion of **long-term economic growth**. By funding space exploration, clean energy, and sustainable technologies, the UC would support the **expansion of global economic potential**.

- **Capital Investment**: The UC would encourage large-scale investments in **space infrastructure, AI research**, and **renewable energy**. Through an advanced system of **smart contracts** and **AI-managed investments**, funding could be channeled into the most promising technologies, ensuring that capital flows efficiently to where it's most needed.

- **Productivity Growth**: Technological progress in fields like **robotics, automation**, and **artificial intelligence** would result in **higher productivity** across industries. The **space race** could serve as a platform for **technological leaps** that trickle down to Earth economies, creating new industries, reducing costs, and increasing the standard of living for billions.

C. Inflation Control and Monetary Policy

The UC system's ability to **adjust its money supply** based on **resource-backed assets** (like space mining) provides an interesting alternative to traditional **monetary policy**. The supply of UC would be tightly controlled through **blockchain** technology and managed by AI systems to ensure that inflation remains stable.

- **Resource-Backed Value**: As space resources are extracted and processed, they would increase the supply of goods that back the UC, creating a natural **anti-inflationary pressure**. This ensures that UC maintains value over time, unlike fiat currencies which can lose value due to excessive printing.

- **Macroeconomic Stability**: The AI system could optimize the **supply of UC** in response to economic indicators, reducing the risk of inflationary spirals or recessions. As global economic conditions change—due to technological breakthroughs or space exploration milestones—AI would automatically adjust monetary supply and interest rates, ensuring **macro stability**.

D. Global Inequality and Economic Redistribution

The Universal Currency presents a unique opportunity to address **global inequality**. Traditionally, wealth is concentrated in certain nations or regions due to access to resources, technology, and capital. The UC system's ability to provide **equal access** to financial resources can help redistribute wealth on a **global scale**.

- **Universal Basic Income (UBI)**: As a core feature of the UC system, UBI could be used to provide all citizens with a basic standard of living, ensuring that the benefits of space exploration and technological progress are **equitably distributed**. This would reduce **poverty** and address disparities in access to resources.

- **Inclusive Growth**: The UC system could drive more inclusive economic growth by ensuring that **developing nations** have access to the same financial tools and opportunities as developed nations. This would enable the **global south** to participate more actively in the global economy and benefit from space resources and technologies.

IV. Conclusion: The Future of the Universal Currency

The **Universal Currency** system represents a bold new economic frontier, blending both **microeconomic efficiency** and **macroeconomic stability**. By leveraging **AI, blockchain technology**, and **space resources**, this currency could revolutionize the way we think about global trade, economic growth, and inequality. The key to its success will be its ability to **balance technological progress** with **equitable wealth distribution**, creating a system that benefits all of humanity, regardless of where they live—on Earth or beyond.

By aligning **economic incentives**, fostering **global collaboration**, and encouraging **sustainable growth**, the UC system could help usher in a new era of human prosperity, unlocking the full potential of the **space age** while addressing many of Earth's most pressing challenges.

Chapter 7: Implementing Solutions

To implement the grand vision of a modern, space-driven economy in the real world, there would be an array of challenges to overcome. These challenges span from technological hurdles to geopolitical cooperation, economic restructuring, and societal adaptation. That said, I can offer 100 practical examples or steps to begin implementing aspects of this economic system, with an emphasis on technological advancement, financial systems, space exploration, and sustainable development.

1. Universal Digital Devices & Connectivity

1. **Develop a universal digital device** (smartphone/tablet) that integrates global communication, finance, and space exploration news.
2. **Partner with SpaceX** to provide global internet coverage via Starlink for universal access to banking and educational resources.
3. **Establish an international mobile payment system** integrated with digital currencies.
4. **Develop blockchain-based mobile banking platforms** for transparent and efficient cross-border transactions.
5. **Create mobile apps for universal basic income distribution**, ensuring equitable financial access to all citizens.

2. Space Race & Technology Incentives

6. **Launch an international space competition** similar to the original Space Race, where nations or private companies compete to solve specific space-related challenges.
7. **Use tax incentives for private space ventures** to lower the cost of satellite launches.

8. **Develop space tourism industries** with companies like Blue Origin or Virgin Galactic, with the goal of eventually reducing the cost of space exploration.
9. **Create space mining ventures** to extract valuable resources (like rare earth metals) from asteroids.
10. **Set up international collaboration on space research** via public-private partnerships (e.g., NASA and private companies working on Mars rovers).

3. Advanced Education & Research Investment

11. **Fund new educational programs** focused on astrophysics, space exploration, and engineering in developing countries.
12. **Expand online education platforms** (e.g., Coursera, edX) to offer free space-related courses globally.
13. **Establish a global "Moonshot Fund" for space research** to foster collaboration on advanced space missions.
14. **Incentivize private corporations** (like Google or Amazon) to donate to space-related educational initiatives.
15. **Introduce advanced financial literacy programs** into schools worldwide, teaching the principles of modern economics, blockchain, and space financing.

4. Sustainable Energy Development

16. **Increase investment in nuclear fusion energy** research, with partnerships between governments and private sectors like ITER.
17. **Expand solar power research** to develop more efficient and scalable space-based solar panels that could eventually power Earth.

18. **Establish nuclear energy plants** on the Moon or Mars to produce energy for space colonies.
19. **Invest in artificial photosynthesis technologies** that could provide clean energy on Earth.
20. **Support the development of space-based power stations** to beam solar energy back to Earth via microwaves.

5. Deregulating Trade & Technology Sharing

21. **Form an international trade federation** to streamline global supply chains and remove barriers for space-based industries.
22. **Release trade secrets related to space exploration** to allow greater cooperation in space ventures.
23. **Deregulate satellite communications** to allow private companies to offer faster and cheaper global internet.
24. **Establish cross-border technology incubators** to allow faster transfer of innovations between countries.
25. **Encourage collaborative international open-source space projects** to break down barriers in the development of new space technologies.

6. Communication & Language Barriers

26. **Develop real-time language translation software** for international space research collaboration.
27. **Integrate AI-powered communication platforms** that break down barriers for astronauts from different countries to collaborate.
28. **Standardize space mission protocols** across countries, ensuring that every

astronaut, regardless of language, can understand instructions.

29. **Develop space-based AI systems** that act as multilingual communication hubs for interplanetary exploration.
30. **Fund language education initiatives** globally to promote inter-national dialogue on scientific research.

7. Building Infrastructure in Space

31. **Develop Mars habitats** using 3D printing technology, sourcing materials from the Martian surface.
32. **Establish a permanent human presence on the Moon** to serve as a launching point for future space exploration.
33. **Invest in space elevators** to reduce the cost of transporting materials between Earth and low-Earth orbit.
34. **Build interplanetary transport systems** using reusable spacecraft (e.g., SpaceX's Starship).
35. **Create orbital docking stations** for spacecraft to refuel, resupply, and change crews.

8. Space Military & Security

36. **Create an international space defense force** to protect satellite infrastructure and prevent space warfare.
37. **Develop anti-satellite weapon countermeasures** to ensure the protection of valuable space assets.
38. **Implement space law** to ensure peaceful use of outer space and prevent militarization.
39. **Establish a global space security alliance**, similar to NATO, to defend against potential space threats.

40. **Use AI-driven monitoring systems** to track space debris and prevent accidents.

9. Healthcare and Technology for Space Travel

41. **Fund research into long-duration space missions** to address psychological and physiological challenges.
42. **Develop artificial gravity systems** to simulate Earth-like conditions on spacecraft and space colonies.
43. **Invest in advanced telemedicine** that allows doctors on Earth to treat astronauts during deep-space missions.
44. **Establish interplanetary medical research stations** to study the effects of space travel on human health.
45. **Research space-adapted pharmaceuticals** that can aid in the physical health of astronauts on long voyages.

10. Artificial Intelligence & Automation

46. **Integrate AI into economic decision-making platforms** to increase efficiency in markets and reduce costs.
47. **Deploy AI in manufacturing** to automate processes and increase the scale and speed of production for space-related goods.
48. **Use AI-powered robots** for space exploration, reducing the need for human presence on dangerous missions.
49. **Develop AI-driven market analysis tools** to predict trends in the space economy and optimize investment strategies.
50. **Create automated supply chain systems** that operate on Earth and in space, ensuring goods are produced and distributed efficiently.

11. Capital Investment in Space Businesses

51. **Create space venture capital funds** to finance private space exploration companies.
52. **Offer tax incentives for space startups** to encourage private sector involvement in space exploration.
53. **Establish a global space stock market** where investors can trade shares in space companies and technologies.
54. **Launch a space commodity exchange** for trading resources like lunar water, space minerals, and Mars-based agricultural products.
55. **Invest in space-based startups** that specialize in asteroid mining, space tourism, and space agriculture.

12. Developing Space Habitation & Real Estate

56. **Sell or lease land on Mars** to private companies or nations for the development of settlements.
57. **Create Moon-based real estate ventures**, offering land to companies that want to develop research stations or factories.
58. **Establish international space property laws** to govern ownership of space resources and land.
59. **Create sustainable space-based agriculture systems** that use hydroponics and solar energy for food production.
60. **Develop space tourism hotels** that offer vacations on the Moon or low-Earth orbit stations.

13. Building a Space Economy

61. **Develop space-based manufacturing facilities** that create materials using lunar or Martian resources.

62. **Create a lunar economy** focused on mining Helium-3 for fusion energy.
63. **Launch a global space trade network** to exchange goods and services between Earth and space colonies.
64. **Establish space supply chains** that source raw materials from asteroids, the Moon, or Mars.
65. **Offer tax breaks to space companies** that build Earth-to-orbit transport systems.

14. Space Exploration Media & Public Engagement

66. **Create space-focused media campaigns** to raise awareness about the importance of space exploration for economic development.
67. **Launch a global space documentary series** to engage the public in space exploration.
68. **Create space-based reality TV shows** to bring the excitement of space exploration into people's homes.
69. **Sponsor space-themed events and festivals** to inspire youth to pursue careers in science, technology, and space.
70. **Develop a global space knowledge-sharing platform** where individuals, companies, and governments can exchange space research.

15. Global Healthcare Initiatives

71. **Develop space-compatible medical technologies** (e.g., advanced prosthetics, zero-gravity medical equipment).
72. **Expand global healthcare networks** by connecting rural areas to advanced telemedicine systems.

73. **Create global healthcare research hubs** dedicated to solving health problems related to space travel and zero-gravity.
74. **Develop vaccine delivery systems** that can be used in remote or space environments.
75. **Incentivize private companies to innovate** in the field of medical technology, ensuring fast adaptation for space missions.

16. Finance & Investment Systems

76. **Create a universal basic income system** funded through global wealth taxes and space-related profits.
77. **Establish interplanetary banks** that manage the economies of Earth, the Moon, Mars, and beyond.
78. **Launch a space-backed cryptocurrency** that acts as a universal currency for space-related transactions.
79. **Invest in financial algorithms** that predict and optimize space markets, from resource mining to space tourism.
80. **Set up universal credit systems** to allow everyone access to loans, financing, and space investments.

17. Automation in Agriculture & Food Security

81. **Invest in agricultural robots** to automate food production in space colonies.
82. **Develop space-based food production systems** that utilize advanced hydroponics and vertical farming.
83. **Use AI to optimize crop yields** on Earth and in space colonies.
84. **Create sustainable farming systems** that can be easily replicated on other planets.
85. **Develop a space agriculture institute** to study and implement space-adapted farming techniques.

18. Public Engagement in Space & Science

86. **Create a global "Space Awareness Month"** to raise public interest in space exploration and its economic potential.
87. **Offer incentives for space-related educational achievements**, like scholarships or jobs in the space industry.
88. **Use social media platforms** to promote the latest space exploration discoveries and innovations.
89. **Encourage public participation** in citizen science programs focused on space exploration.
90. **Host live space exploration broadcasts**, similar to the Apollo missions, to engage the global population.

19. Political & Legal Framework

91. **Develop an international space treaty** that outlines the legal framework for colonizing space and distributing resources.
92. **Implement space-specific taxes** to fund international space exploration programs.
93. **Establish space diplomacy** to resolve international disputes over resources and land ownership in space.
94. **Create space governance models** for interplanetary nations or colonies.
95. **Establish an international space regulatory body** to ensure fair and sustainable practices.

20. Health & Well-being for the Future

96. **Invest in mental health programs** for astronauts, ensuring their well-being on long-term missions.
97. **Support research on aging in space** to address the impact of space travel on human lifespan.

98. **Introduce universal health care** on space colonies to ensure the well-being of all inhabitants.
99. **Create space-based fitness systems** to prevent muscle loss and maintain astronaut health.
100.   **Develop genetic and bioengineering research** to help humans adapt better to the challenges of space travel.

Chapter 8: The Metrics of Implementing Solutions

1. Metrics for the "Great Conversion" (Chapter 1)

The concept of the Great Conversion involves optimizing resource allocation across multiple industries (energy, space exploration, etc.). You'd typically look at metrics like:

- **Energy Conversion Efficiency**:

  - Solar Efficiency: The average efficiency of solar cells today is about 15-22% (depending on technology).

  - Cost per Watt: For solar power, the cost has dropped from around $70 per watt in the 1970s to about $0.25-0.50 per watt in 2025.

- **Energy Consumption**:

  - Global Energy Consumption: As of 2021, the world used about 600 exajoules of energy.

  - Fossil Fuel Dependency: Fossil fuels still account for approximately 80% of global energy consumption.

2. Metrics for Subsistence Agriculture (Chapter 2)

For measuring agricultural efficiency, production costs, and labor utilization in a subsistence agriculture model:

- **Agricultural Output per Acre:**

- o Modern yield rates for crops like corn: about 175-200 bushels per acre in the U.S.

  - o Food Security Index: The global Food Security Index scores countries based on their food affordability, availability, and quality.

- **Labor Cost Efficiency**:

  - o Typical labor cost for agricultural workers: U.S. average agricultural worker wage is about $14 per hour.

  - o Automation vs. Manual Labor: The use of robotics in farming has been shown to reduce costs by 30-50% over time.

3. Metrics for Industry (Chapter 3)

Key financial metrics for industrialization and automation:

- **Production Costs & Automation Savings**:

  - o Robotic Automation: The cost of robotic automation systems in manufacturing can range from $25,000 to $250,000 per robot, but the savings in labor costs over time can be substantial.

  - o Labor Productivity: In the U.S., labor productivity has been increasing at an average rate of about 2-3% annually.

- **Space Industry Financials**:

- o SpaceX's estimated valuation: As of 2024, SpaceX is valued at around $150 billion.

- o Costs for Space Transport: A Falcon 9 launch costs around $62 million per launch, which is significantly lower than previous rocket costs (around $450 million per launch for the Space Shuttle).

4. Metrics for Real Estate in Space (Chapter 4)

Metrics for space real estate would involve resource costs, industry investments, and future projections:

- **Cost of Space Exploration**:

  - o NASA's 2025 Budget for Space Exploration: Estimated at around $25 billion for the Artemis Program.

  - o Mars Colonization Cost Estimates: The cost of a Mars mission is estimated at $50-100 billion for initial stages, with ongoing costs running into hundreds of billions over decades.

- **Land Acquisition Costs in Space**:

  - o As no clear legal framework currently exists for the ownership of celestial bodies, space land ownership remains an unclear financial area. However, private entities may begin to invest in technologies that help in resource extraction from bodies like the Moon and Mars.

Charts and Data (Hypothetical Example)

Below are some examples of the types of charts or financial data that could be useful for understanding the economic implications of the topics discussed:

1. Energy Conversion Efficiency (Chart)

Year	Solar Efficiency (%)	Cost per Watt ($)	Total Global Energy Consumption (Exajoules)
1970	6%	70	400
2000	12%	5	500
2025	18%	0.25-0.50	600

2. Global Agriculture Data (Chart)

Country	Crop Yield per Acre (Bushels)	Labor Cost (Hourly Wage $)	Automation Adoption Rate (%)
U.S.	175-200	14	25
India	100-120	3	10
China	150-175	6	15

3. Space Industry Investment (Chart)

Company	Estimated Valuation ($ Billion)	Cost per Launch ($ Million)	Annual Investment in Space Exploration ($ Billion)
SpaceX	150	62	2-5
Blue Origin	10	80	1-2
NASA	25	450 (Space Shuttle Era)	25

4. Mars Colonization Cost (Chart)

Stage	Estimated Cost ($ Billion)
Initial Mission & Setup	50-100
Ongoing Missions & Habitat	10-50 per year
Resource Extraction	20-50 annually
Terraforming Research	100-200

5. Space Real Estate in the Future (Hypothetical Example)

Cost to Colonize Mars

- **Transport Costs**: Transporting cargo and humans could cost anywhere from $5 million to $50 million per launch depending on the technology.

- **Habitat Setup**: A sustainable habitat on Mars might cost an estimated $10 billion initially for setup.

- **Resource Mining**: Mining operations on Mars for Helium-3 or water could cost $500 million to $2 billion, with high returns expected due to the scarcity of these resources on Earth.

Other Key Financial Metrics

- **Return on Investment (ROI)** for Space-related companies: For example, SpaceX, with its reusable rockets and satellite launch services, sees a significant ROI due to cost reductions in space transport.

- **Risk and Insurance Costs**: Space missions often involve large insurance premiums. For instance, the cost of insuring a space mission may range between $20 million to $100 million depending on the mission's scale.

Conclusion

The framework provided offers a detailed view of how you might approach financial analysis of space exploration, industry development, and real estate in space. The cost metrics for space exploration, energy production, subsistence agriculture, and industrialization help in conceptualizing the vast scale of these projects.

Chapter 9: Transportation

The Global Transportation System for the Space Age: Envisioning an Interplanetary Network

In order to meet the ambitious goals of modern economics outlined above, a state-of-the-art, multi-tiered transportation system must be developed. This system would be grounded in current technological advancements and future innovations, combining global Earth-bound infrastructure with space transportation networks that can facilitate the needs of humanity's expansion into space, particularly Mars. The system would provide not only physical transportation for people, cargo, and data but also establish a seamless connection between terrestrial and space exploration efforts.

Key Components of the Global Transportation System

1. Earth-to-Space Transit Infrastructure

The Earth-to-Space transit network is the cornerstone of humanity's path into the future. This will involve a combination of spaceports, rocket systems, and emerging technologies like space elevators, cargo shuttles, and commercial spaceflights.

- **Spaceports:** Like airports today, spaceports would serve as hubs for space travel, acting as launch points for missions to various celestial destinations. These hubs would need to be distributed across continents and could even be located in less densely populated areas to reduce risks to urban populations.

- **Reusable Rockets:** Inspired by current private space agencies like SpaceX, reusable rockets and spacecraft would become the primary mode of Earth-to-space travel. These rockets would be launched from various spaceports around the globe, equipped to return to Earth after their missions for refueling and re-use, making the transport process more efficient and affordable.

- **Space Elevators:** As an eventual long-term solution, space elevators could be developed to replace rocket launches. A space elevator would be a massive structure stretching from Earth's surface to geostationary orbit, allowing for cost-effective, sustainable transport of goods and people into space without the need for conventional rockets.

2. Solar System Transportation Network

Once in space, the transport network will consist of a sophisticated system of spacecraft, propulsion technologies, and stations designed to ensure smooth transit across the solar system.

- **Spacecraft Design:** New spacecraft would be optimized for long-term space travel, offering varying sizes depending on their purpose—some for cargo transport, others for crewed missions. These would be powered by a combination of solar energy, nuclear fission/fusion propulsion, and ion drives, enabling faster and more efficient travel.

- **Cargo Vessels:** These vessels would transport goods between Earth, lunar colonies, Mars, and potentially other space stations or moons. Using advanced cryogenic storage systems and automated docking protocols, they would handle everything from mining materials to life-sustaining resources like food and medical supplies.

- **Space Stations and Docking Ports:** A network of space stations would be strategically placed to support a wide range of needs—scientific research, refueling, trade hubs, and even tourist facilities. These stations would facilitate re-supply, maintenance, and transit across the solar system, with Mars, the Moon, and possibly asteroids serving as key waypoints.

- **Mars-to-Earth Linkages:** Regular transport of personnel and resources between Earth and Mars would be central to establishing a colony on Mars. Technologies for safe, efficient interplanetary travel would need to be developed, such as advanced propulsion systems (e.g., nuclear thermal propulsion, fusion-powered rockets) that can reduce travel time and ensure the safety of astronauts on the long journey.

3. Communication and Data Transfer System

Communication between Earth and space, as well as between different space stations and colonies, will be key to supporting this global transportation system.

- **Laser Communication:** With the vast distances involved, optical laser-based communication could replace radio waves for faster, higher-bandwidth data transmission between space vessels and Earth. This system would enable near-instantaneous communication between space stations, spacecraft, and control centers on Earth.

- **Quantum Communication:** Emerging technologies like quantum encryption and communication could be used to secure data and communications across space, ensuring that vital information (such as trade transactions, military operations, and scientific discoveries) remains protected.

- **Global Network:** On Earth, a unified communication network would allow seamless interaction between space and terrestrial operations, driven by the latest in 5G/6G technologies and satellite communication systems. This would keep the flow of goods, people, and information constant, preventing delays or logistical bottlenecks in the system.

4. Global Earth-Based Transportation System for Space-Related Goods and Services

The Earth-based transportation infrastructure must adapt to the new era of space exploration by supporting the launch and storage of cargo and passengers.

- **High-Speed Ground Transport:** To facilitate swift access to spaceports, the global transportation system would incorporate next-generation hyperloop or maglev (magnetic levitation) systems, drastically reducing the time it takes to transport goods and people to spaceports from anywhere on Earth.

- **Automated Cargo Systems:** Drones, autonomous trucks, and AI-powered logistics systems would facilitate the movement of materials to spaceports, ensuring that cargo shipments are efficiently managed.

- **Intermodal Transit Hubs:** These hubs would serve as transition points between ground and space transportation. For example, a person traveling from a remote region would take high-speed ground transport to an intermodal hub, where they could board a space shuttle or spacecraft for their journey into orbit or beyond.

5. International Regulatory Bodies and Governance Structures

To manage and oversee this vast global and space transportation network, new international institutions would be required.

- **Global Trade Federation:** A trade federation would be established to regulate and promote trade between Earth and other planets. This body would coordinate the transportation of goods, enforce safety and security measures, and ensure that all activities comply with international law.

- **Space Military and Defense Coordination:** Given the importance of protecting vital infrastructure in space, a space-based defense force would need to be established. It would be responsible for defending spaceports, space stations, and the space lanes between Earth, Mars, and beyond from potential threats, whether from rogue states, private actors, or extraterrestrial dangers.

- **Unified International Bank System:** With the introduction of a universal digital currency, an international bank would be necessary to oversee interplanetary transactions and manage the financial infrastructure supporting the new space economy. It would play a role in regulating trade, investments, and the growth of interplanetary businesses.

6. Environmental and Sustainability Considerations

As humanity moves into space, the transportation system must be designed with sustainability in mind, reducing its carbon footprint both on Earth and in space.

- **Green Propulsion Technologies:** The use of nuclear fusion or solar sails for spacecraft propulsion would ensure that emissions are minimized during transit across the solar system. Recycling systems on spacecraft and space stations would also ensure minimal waste and resource consumption.

- **Space Habitat Development:** To sustain long-term space exploration, habitats on Mars and the Moon would need to rely on closed-loop life support systems, renewable energy sources, and sustainable food production systems, reducing dependence on Earth for supplies.

Conclusion: A Unified Vision of Progress

The transportation system described here integrates cutting-edge technologies and interplanetary infrastructure to create a fully integrated, global-to-space transportation network. This system would enable the growth of humanity's presence beyond Earth, encourage technological innovation, and fuel economic and scientific advancements on an unprecedented scale. By uniting the efforts of governments, corporations, and global institutions, this system would not only fulfill the goals of modern economics but also set humanity on a path toward becoming an interplanetary species.

To envision the **Global Transportation System for the Space Age** in terms of economic principles, it's important to analyze how **efficiency, scalability, market creation**, and **international collaboration** would transform the global economy and space exploration efforts. This system would need to incorporate not just technological innovation, but also the economic mechanisms that would incentivize investment, optimize resource allocation, and ensure long-term sustainability.

1. Earth-to-Space Transit Infrastructure: Economic Incentives and Investment Strategies

The **Earth-to-Space transit network** will require significant upfront capital investment, but the **economies of scale** and the resulting **return on investment (ROI)** will make it profitable in the long run. As the infrastructure scales, the cost of transportation will decrease, making space access accessible to more players in the economy.

- **Public-Private Partnerships (PPP):** Governments could partner with private corporations (such as SpaceX, Blue Origin, etc.) to develop the essential technologies like **reusable rockets, spaceports,** and **space elevators**. By offering tax incentives, subsidies, and government-backed guarantees, these partnerships could drive down initial costs, while enabling private players to capitalize on space-related business opportunities.

- **Price Elasticity of Demand (PED):** As transport costs decrease (with reusable rockets or the advent of space elevators), the **price elasticity of demand** for space-based services—ranging from tourism to cargo delivery—would increase. As space travel becomes more affordable, we would expect **higher demand** for both goods and services in space, fueling further economic expansion.

- **Network Externalities:** The more spaceports, elevators, and transportation routes established globally, the more valuable the system becomes for everyone. With a **global space transportation system**, the marginal utility of each new user (whether individual or corporate) increases as the network grows. This leads to network externalities that benefit early adopters, especially with **multimodal transportation hubs** linking Earth to space.

---

2. Solar System Transportation Network: Market Creation and Innovation

Once beyond Earth, the **solar system transportation network** needs to operate on principles that encourage **technological innovation, market competition**, and **collaboration between space-faring nations**.

- **Cost-Effective Supply Chains:** In the initial stages, large-scale **space cargo vessels** and **Mars-to-Earth linkages** would primarily serve governmental needs (e.g., scientific research, infrastructure). However, as technologies mature, **commercial interests** will enter the market, reducing the cost of shipping and enabling the development of **supply chains** between Earth, the Moon, and Mars.

- **Cost-Benefit Analysis:** As the technology to build **space stations** and **refueling hubs** in orbit or on the Moon advances, the economic principle of **marginal utility** suggests that the cost of supplying materials to these hubs (using energy-efficient propulsion technologies such as **solar sails** and **ion drives**) will eventually fall to the point where **private companies** and **independent entrepreneurs** can profitably manage interplanetary freight.

- **Global Trade and Comparative Advantage:** As lunar and Martian colonies develop, the principle of **comparative advantage** will come into play. For example, Mars might be more suitable for **mining certain resources**, while Earth can focus on **advanced manufacturing**. Space transportation infrastructure will be necessary to enable this **interplanetary**

trade in raw materials, manufactured goods, and specialized technologies.

---

3. Communication and Data Transfer System: The Role of Digital Economies

The introduction of **laser and quantum communication technologies** represents a **key pillar** in supporting the **data transfer systems** necessary for efficient operation of the space economy.

- **Information as a Commodity:** Fast, secure, and high-capacity communication channels between Earth and space will lower **transaction costs**, making it easier for space-based businesses to operate. These businesses could include **telemedicine** services for astronauts, **space tourism** bookings, **financial transactions** between Mars and Earth, and **remote labor** from space stations to Earth-based firms. The economic principle of **digital economies** will support the growth of entire industries based on real-time data exchange.

- **Network Effects and Economic Integration: Quantum encryption** and **global data connectivity** will enable the **seamless integration** of space stations and colonies into the global economic system. As communication technology improves, space-based **financial markets** will emerge, giving rise to new forms of space-based trading platforms that connect Earth and space economies.

- **Global Network Economy:** From an economic standpoint, the communication network enables a **global economy of scale**. By enabling real-time, **cross-planetary communication**, the interplanetary economy will flourish through **cooperative ventures**, increasing **efficiency** and **increasing international trade**.

---

4. Earth-Based Transportation System for Space-Related Goods and Services: Logistics and Efficiency

The **Earth-based transport system** would need to evolve rapidly to support the **new space economy** by reducing logistical friction between terrestrial and space-bound goods and services.

- **Economies of Speed and Scale:** The deployment of **high-speed transport** (e.g., **maglev** or **hyperloop**) to spaceports will drastically reduce the costs of **last-mile delivery** from urban centers to spaceports. With the ability to rapidly transport large amounts of materials and people, economies of scale will increase. **Cost minimization** through automation and AI-based logistics systems will create a **supply chain** model that can scale from Earth-based resources to space-based infrastructure.

- **Capital Mobility and Investment Flow:** The growing demand for **autonomous cargo systems**, like **drones and AI-powered logistics**, will spark a wave of **capital investments** in transportation tech. Investors in **robotics** and **AI systems** will create more efficient methods for intermodal transportation that significantly reduces the cost of delivering resources to spaceports. This capital flow will boost economic growth both on Earth and in space.

- **Microeconomic Optimization:** Space-related services and goods would be managed under efficient **supply chain economics**, using AI-based **optimization algorithms** that can handle the global-to-space transition with **minimal waste**. Local economic systems will specialize in producing either **raw materials** or **space-faring technologies** for the interplanetary trade, ensuring **efficiency** in **resource allocation**.

5. International Regulatory Bodies and Governance Structures: Managing Interplanetary Trade and Security

The **global governance structures** required for managing the interconnected Earth-to-space economy must promote **international cooperation** and **economic stability**.

- **International Monetary Systems:** The establishment of an **international digital currency** would be critical for reducing **transaction costs** and **currency exchange friction** between planets. A **unified financial system** under a **global trade federation** would simplify trade between Earth and Mars, eliminating the need for complex financial arrangements and enabling **streamlined cross-planetary**

commerce. This could take the form of a **universal space economy** that operates on **blockchain** or other **distributed ledger technologies** to ensure transparency and secure transactions.

- **Trade Liberalization and Comparative Advantage:** By facilitating **free trade** between Earth, the Moon, Mars, and future colonies, the space economy would benefit from **trade liberalization**—reducing tariffs, market restrictions, and ensuring that each celestial body can focus on producing goods and services where it holds a **comparative advantage**. For example, Mars could specialize in producing **mining-based products**, while Earth provides **advanced manufacturing**, **medicine**, and **technology**.

- **Security and the Space Economy:** The creation of **space defense** forces will have economic implications, especially for the protection of key infrastructure like spaceports, space stations, and resource transport lanes. From an economic standpoint, the cost of **military investment** in space security would be balanced by the **economic stability** these forces provide by protecting critical **trade routes** and **resource access**.

Conclusion: A Globally Integrated Space Economy

The development of a **Global Transportation System for the Space Age** would harness economic principles like **efficiency, comparative advantage,** and **network externalities** to create a seamless interplanetary network. **Public-private partnerships**, **global regulatory bodies**, and **trade federations** would be essential for **scaling** technologies and encouraging **cross-border cooperation**. This network will not only expand the frontiers of human exploration but also act as an engine for **global economic growth**, transforming humanity into an interplanetary species capable of thriving on Earth and beyond.

Chapter 10: Security, Law Enforcement, and Military

Security System and Law Enforcement Initiative for the Modern Economic and Space Age Vision

As humanity transitions into a future where space exploration and interplanetary commerce are crucial to the global economy, robust **security and law enforcement** structures must be developed to ensure the safety of both Earth and outer space endeavors. The principles guiding this security system should be rooted in **international collaboration, global governance**, and the principles of **democracy** while safeguarding **economic stability, human rights**, and **technological integrity**.

1. Global Security Framework for Earth and Space

The modern economic and technological landscape requires an overarching security system that integrates terrestrial and space operations. This system would address both traditional security threats on Earth and the emerging needs of space security.

Key Components:

1. **International Space Security Coalition (ISSC):**

   o **Mandate**: To oversee space-based security operations, ensuring that space exploration, research, and commercial activities are carried out within the boundaries of international law, particularly the

Outer Space Treaty and **new space governance frameworks**.

- o **Jurisdiction**: ISSC would have authority over both the defense of space-based infrastructure (like space stations and satellites) and the **safeguarding of space trade routes** between Earth, the Moon, Mars, and beyond.

- o **Security Operations**: Establish joint space defense and law enforcement agencies with **space-faring nations**, such as the **United Nations Space Security Council (UNSSC)**, to regulate space militarization, resource mining, and space trade.

2. **Earth-Based Security Network (EBSN)**:

- o **Purpose**: To protect Earth-based infrastructure that supports space exploration, including **spaceports**, **launch facilities**, and **global transportation networks**.

- o **Integration with International Security Forces**: The EBSN will operate in collaboration with existing global law enforcement and military agencies, including the **Interpol** and **UN Peacekeeping Forces**, to secure **trade routes, information flow**, and **public safety**.

- o **Technological Oversight**: Ensure that sensitive technologies—such as **fusion reactors, nuclear propulsion** systems, and **AI-driven space systems**—are protected from cyber threats, espionage, and sabotage.

3. **Interplanetary Defense Forces (IDF)**:

    o   **Mandate**: To establish an **offensive and defensive military presence** in space, ensuring the security of space stations, trade lanes, and colonies on Mars and the Moon.

    o   **Key Technologies**: The IDF would employ **satellite-based missile defense systems, drone fleets**, and **space-based autonomous weapons systems** to prevent threats from rogue states or private actors.

    o   **Legal Framework**: The IDF would operate under a **global space law** that adheres to the peaceful exploration mandate of the **Outer Space Treaty** while enforcing **space security**.

    o   **Collaboration**: Working in tandem with **private space companies** and **research institutions** to monitor space activities and enforce regulatory measures for **space debris management** and **resource utilization**.

---

2. Law Enforcement and Regulatory Bodies

In this new interplanetary society, law enforcement must bridge the gap between **Earth-based law** and

space law to ensure the rule of law governs the development of new economic systems in space.

Key Components:

1. **Interplanetary Law Enforcement Agency (ILEA):**

   - **Role**: The ILEA would operate across both **terrestrial and extraterrestrial jurisdictions** to monitor **criminal activity** and enforce **international space law**. This includes piracy, illegal mining, unauthorized space station activities, and space-based terrorism.

   - **Space Crime Investigation**: A specialized **space crimes unit** would be formed to deal with criminal cases like **data theft, smuggling of illicit materials**, and **theft of intellectual property** from space-based corporations.

   - **International Legal Framework**: The agency would collaborate with the **United Nations Office for Outer Space Affairs (UNOOSA)** and space law scholars to establish the **legal systems** for **property rights in space, interplanetary treaties**, and **trade agreements**.

2. **Universal Cybersecurity Council (UCC):**

   - **Purpose**: To regulate and monitor **cybersecurity threats** that could jeopardize the functioning of the **global space economy**. As space missions become more reliant on **AI**, **quantum computing**, and **digital payment systems**, this body would oversee the protection of critical space infrastructure from **cyberattacks**.

- **Cybercrime Investigation**: Establishing a global **cybersecurity task force** with expertise in AI, quantum encryption, and blockchain technology to secure the **digital currency** used for interplanetary trade.

- **International Partnerships**: The UCC would work with **private tech companies**, **security firms**, and **space agencies** to ensure a coordinated response to cyber threats, with penalties for breaches that jeopardize the global economy or space missions.

3. **Global Trade Federation (GTF) Enforcement**:

- **Mandate**: The GTF would ensure the **smooth operation of interplanetary trade** and **enforce trade regulations**. This body would deal with customs enforcement, regulatory violations, and trade disputes between Earth and colonies like Mars and the Moon.

- **Regulatory Oversight**: The GTF will regulate the flow of goods between planets, ensuring that only legally obtained resources (such as minerals from asteroids or the Moon) are traded and that space-related goods meet international safety standards.

- o **Monitoring**: The **interplanetary customs enforcement** team would use **AI-powered drones**, **space surveillance systems**, and **satellite tracking** to monitor cargo ships and space freighters.

- o **Dispute Resolution**: In case of trade disagreements, the GTF would serve as an **arbitration body** to resolve disputes according to interplanetary trade laws and **democratic principles**.

---

3. Cyber and Physical Security Systems for Space and Earth Operations

To support the rapid expansion of space activities and ensure the protection of critical infrastructure, **advanced security systems** will be required.

Key Components:

1. **AI-Enhanced Surveillance Systems**:

   - o **Space Surveillance**: Leveraging **artificial intelligence (AI)** and **machine learning**, this system would track and monitor space debris, satellites, and cargo vessels in orbit. AI algorithms could automatically detect **anomalies** or

unauthorized activities in space and trigger immediate action.

- o **Earth Surveillance**: On Earth, AI-driven systems would be used to monitor activities at **spaceports**, **launch facilities**, and **research stations**. **Predictive analytics** would be employed to anticipate **threats** and deploy **preemptive measures**.

2. **Satellite-Based Threat Detection**:

- o **Advanced Early Warning**: Space-based sensors and **satellite constellations** would be integrated into the defense network to provide real-time updates on **missile launches**, **space piracy**, and other threats.

- o **Laser and Kinetic Defense**: The space-based defense system would be equipped with **laser weapons** or **kinetic interceptors** to counter potential threats, such as **space debris**, rogue satellites, or missile attacks on space infrastructure.

3. **Biometric Security and Identity Management**:

- o As space exploration expands, identity management will be vital. The **universal biometric system** would be established to identify personnel traveling to space and accessing space-based facilities. Using **iris scans, DNA verification,** and **fingerprint technology**, biometric data would ensure the security of critical systems and prevent unauthorized access.

4. **Blockchain for Security**:

    o **Space Asset Management**: Blockchain technology could be used to **secure space trade transactions** and protect intellectual property rights in space. By decentralizing **financial transactions** and asset ownership on the blockchain, this system will reduce the risk of fraud, piracy, and unauthorized exploitation of space resources.

---

4. Preventive Law Enforcement: Education and Diplomacy

To foster international collaboration and prevent conflicts, **diplomacy** and **public awareness** would play a central role in promoting the rule of law in space.

Key Components:

1. **Space Law Education and Diplomatic Training**:

    o Establish global programs for educating law enforcement officers, diplomats, and corporate leaders on space law, governance structures, and the peaceful uses of outer space.

    o **International Cooperation Initiatives**: Diplomatic missions would focus on ensuring that the **democratic values** that guide Earth's societies are upheld in space. Regular **space treaties** and **diplomatic dialogues** would prevent conflicts and regulate the **militarization of space**.

2. **Global Awareness Campaigns**:

   o   To encourage cooperation and prevent illegal activities, a **public awareness campaign** will highlight the **ethical principles** guiding humanity's journey into space, focusing on **peaceful exploration** and the **responsible use of space resources**.

   o   **Media and Advocacy**: Partner with educational institutions, media outlets, and space agencies to promote **international solidarity** and the shared responsibility of maintaining **space law** for future generations.

Conclusion: A Unified Security Initiative for a Unified Future

The global security system must be both adaptable and dynamic, recognizing the evolving nature of space exploration, international trade, and technological advancements. By integrating **advanced technologies, international cooperation**, and **preventive measures**, this system will protect not only the **economic infrastructure** but also uphold **global peace** and **democratic principles** in the face of unprecedented growth and innovation. Through careful collaboration and robust enforcement mechanisms, humanity can transition from Earth's atmosphere into the cosmos in a safe and responsible manner.

Designing a Military for Space Exploration and Interplanetary Commerce

As humanity embarks on the new frontier of space exploration and interplanetary commerce, a new model of military and security forces will be required. This military will need to safeguard not only Earth's territorial interests but also the growing web of human activities in space. Its focus will be on both defensive and peacekeeping roles, ensuring the security of interplanetary trade routes, space colonies, and technological infrastructures while upholding democratic principles, human rights, and global cooperation.

Here's a conceptual design for such a military:

1. Organizational Structure and Governance

Given the scale and complexity of space operations, the military responsible for safeguarding space will be highly decentralized but operate under a unified global framework. The structure should emphasize cooperation among nations and regions while respecting international treaties and laws governing space.

Space Security Council (SSC):

- An overarching body that includes representatives from all member states, this council will govern military operations in space, ensuring adherence to international agreements, such as the Outer Space Treaty. The SSC will be the decision-making authority for space defense strategies, peacekeeping missions, and international cooperation on space security.

- The SSC will operate within a **Democratic Security Framework**, ensuring that military operations are transparent and subject to review by global governing bodies, safeguarding against misuse of power.

- A **Global Security Alliance** will be established to facilitate multinational collaboration. Each participating nation will maintain its own space military units, but with standardized protocols and shared operational goals.

2. Military Branches and Divisions

Given the unique challenges of space warfare and protection, this military will need specialized branches, each tasked with specific areas of responsibility.

A. Space Defense Force (SDF):

- **Mission:** Protect Earth, orbital infrastructure, and interplanetary trade routes from external threats (e.g., space piracy, asteroids, hostile forces).

- **Core Operations:**

  - **Orbital Defense:** Protection of Earth's orbit, satellites, and space stations from attacks or sabotage, including kinetic and cyber threats.

- o **Planetary Defense Systems:** Development of planetary defense capabilities to guard against asteroid impacts, solar storms, and extraterrestrial threats.

- o **Fleet Operations:** Space-faring fleets capable of interplanetary travel, equipped with advanced propulsion systems and defensive technologies to protect trade routes between Earth and colonies on the Moon, Mars, and beyond.

- o **Cybersecurity Divisions:** Dedicated teams to secure the integrity of all space-based communication, data transfer systems, and autonomous technologies. AI systems for monitoring space infrastructure for vulnerabilities to hacking and malicious interference.

B. Space Peacekeeping Corps (SPC):

- • **Mission:** Ensure the peaceful and lawful use of space, manage disputes, and uphold human rights in space colonies.

- • **Core Operations:**

  - o **Interplanetary Policing:** Enforce international space law, maintain order on space stations, and prevent space-based criminal activities such as piracy, illegal mining, and smuggling of advanced technologies.

  - o **Conflict Mediation and Resolution:** Peacekeeping forces to intervene in conflicts within or between space colonies, preventing violence, ensuring compliance with international treaties, and upholding human rights.

- o **Humanitarian Aid:** Rapid deployment units capable of providing aid in space colonies in the event of a crisis, such as natural disasters, food shortages, or medical emergencies.

C. Space Research and Development Command (SRDC):

- **Mission:** Drive technological innovation for military and civilian purposes while ensuring that technological advancements are used responsibly and safely.

- **Core Operations:**

  - o **Research on Defense Technologies:** Ongoing development of cutting-edge weapons, defensive shields, and communication systems to enhance security and maintain peace in space.

  - o **Ethical AI and Autonomous Systems:** Specialized units dedicated to ensuring that all AI-driven systems and autonomous military units function within ethical guidelines, preserving human rights and decision-making in conflict situations.

  - o **Weapons Control Systems:** Robust international protocols for the use and control of space-based weapons, preventing misuse and ensuring any offensive action is strictly regulated.

3. Strategic Defense Technologies

The evolving nature of space requires cutting-edge technologies that can defend space assets, deter potential aggressors, and protect civilian space endeavors. The following strategic systems will be central to the military's operations:

A. Orbital Defense Platforms:

- These would be specialized stations or satellites equipped with energy-based or kinetic weapons capable of intercepting and neutralizing potential threats, such as rogue satellites, space debris, or hostile spacecraft.

- **Laser Defense Systems:** Advanced directed energy weapons for disabling or disabling spacecraft targeting Earth's satellites and orbital infrastructure.

- **Orbital Shielding:** Defensive shields or fields around critical space infrastructure to protect against impacts from debris or projectiles.

B. Space Combat Fleet:

- **Interplanetary Fleet:** A group of well-equipped spacecraft capable of long-duration missions across the solar system to safeguard trade routes, protect space assets, and deter potential aggressors. These vessels would be outfitted with both defensive and offensive capabilities.

- **Autonomous Drones:** Space-based drones designed for reconnaissance, surveillance, and protection, capable of operating autonomously in space environments to detect and respond to threats in real-time.

C. Advanced Surveillance Systems:

- **Space Surveillance Network:** A global network of sensors, both ground-based and space-based, designed to monitor space traffic, detect hostile activity, and track any foreign objects that could pose a threat to space infrastructure.

- **AI-driven Threat Assessment:** Artificial intelligence capable of analyzing data from a wide range of sources in real-time, identifying potential threats, and coordinating defensive actions.

D. Communications and Encryption Systems:

- **Quantum Communication Systems:** Quantum-encrypted communication to ensure that sensitive military and civilian space communications are secure, preventing hacking and interception by adversaries.

- **AI-powered Cyber Defense:** Constant monitoring of digital infrastructures in space to detect and neutralize cyber-attacks, protecting the technological integrity of space missions and Earth-based operations.

4. Training and International Collaboration

The military designed for space exploration and interplanetary commerce must also prioritize collaboration, transparency, and ethical standards. Training will focus on the following areas:

A. Multi-National Training Programs:

- Space forces will engage in joint exercises and simulations, where multiple nations can collaborate on training operations, develop cooperative defense strategies, and build trust.

- **Virtual Training Simulations:** As much of space is still uncharted, training will include virtual environments that simulate space combat and the management of space assets.

B. Ethical Training:

- All personnel will undergo rigorous training in the principles of **human rights**, **democratic governance**, and **international law**, ensuring that military operations align with the ethical standards guiding this future economy.

- **Cultural Awareness:** Space missions and operations will involve individuals from different national, cultural, and ethical backgrounds. It's essential that personnel are prepared for collaboration, conflict resolution, and ensuring respect for all people involved in space missions, whether they are astronauts, space colonists, or inhabitants of Earth.

5. International Legal Frameworks and Accountability

To ensure global cooperation and prevent military overreach, an international legal framework will be critical. This military must operate under the banner of **global governance** and international law, where decisions are made transparently and with accountability to the international community. The military will:

- Operate within the bounds of the **United Nations Space Committee**, which will oversee all space-related military activities to ensure compliance with space law and the ethical use of military power.

- **Adopt strict arms control regulations** for space-based weapons, ensuring they are used only for defensive purposes or in accordance with international law.

- Promote **democratic oversight** over space military operations, ensuring that military leaders answer to civilian governments and international bodies.

Conclusion: A Military that Protects and Serves

The military model designed for space exploration and interplanetary commerce must be one of cooperation, innovation, and protection. It must defend Earth's interests in space, protect interplanetary commerce, and ensure that the future of humanity's space endeavors is built on principles of peace, stability, and ethical governance. With its focus on international collaboration, advanced technologies, and safeguarding human rights, this military will provide security for the next chapter of humanity's journey in space.

Chapter 11: Modern Healthcare

Designing a healthcare system for this ambitious economic vision requires a robust integration of technological advancement, space exploration, economic theory, and social equity. The healthcare system must reflect these principles of technological innovation, financial inclusion, sustainability, and equity. Here's a conceptual breakdown, incorporating relevant economic examples:

1. Universal Access & Digital Health Networks

In the modern, interconnected global economy you envision, healthcare should be universally accessible through digital platforms. This aligns with the goal of universal financial inclusion through the digital banking system, where an integrated healthcare ecosystem exists on the same device (e.g., a universal iPad/phone).

Economic Example:

- **Platform Economy (Digitalization of Healthcare):** Think of the way companies like **Apple** and **Google** are shaping digital health tools (e.g., health apps, AI-powered diagnostics). By merging healthcare with the digital banking infrastructure, citizens can access health consultations, prescriptions, fitness tracking, and mental health services directly through their devices. This "platform economy" allows for a scalable and efficient distribution of health services, breaking down geographical and financial barriers.

- **Impact on Economic Mobility:** Much like how digital finance enables people in remote areas to participate in the global economy, telemedicine could enable rural or isolated populations to access high-quality care. This enhances human capital and productivity.

2. AI, Automation, & Robotics in Healthcare Delivery

Given the importance of technological advancement in your vision, AI, automation, and robotics would play a pivotal role in improving healthcare outcomes, reducing human labor in routine medical tasks, and optimizing resource allocation. These technologies could handle diagnostics, surgical procedures, patient management, and even personalized treatment plans.

Economic Example:

- **Healthcare AI (Cost-Effectiveness & Efficiency):** Imagine AI tools similar to **IBM Watson Health** or Google's **DeepMind** helping doctors make faster and more accurate diagnoses. This would reduce the cost of healthcare by eliminating human error, improving speed, and minimizing unnecessary treatments. In an economy that prizes efficiency, this could drastically reduce the cost of care (important in a future where public health spending must be sustainable).

- **Robot-Assisted Surgery (Productivity Gains):** The use of robotic systems like **Intuitive Surgical's da Vinci** would allow for faster recovery times, fewer complications, and more efficient use of healthcare workers. Robots could reduce the physical and cognitive load on medical personnel, allowing for better care quality across various economic sectors.

3. Space Exploration & Medical Resource Harvesting

Space exploration could serve as both a resource frontier and a catalyst for developing new medical technologies. By accessing space resources such as asteroids, we could mine rare materials used for medical purposes or find new substances with health benefits.

Economic Example:

- **Astro-mining (Resource Scarcity in Healthcare):** Just as the discovery of new resources during the Age of Exploration helped stimulate economic growth, space exploration could address future resource scarcity. Mining asteroids for rare minerals needed in medical devices or pharmaceuticals would secure a future supply of vital resources for the healthcare sector.

- **Space-based Research (Pharmaceutical Innovation):** Research in microgravity environments can lead to breakthroughs in drug development, protein synthesis, and biotechnology. Pharmaceutical companies would compete to develop novel treatments based on space research, driving innovation, lowering costs, and increasing supply.

4. Sustainability & Green Healthcare Solutions

Given the vision of sustainability, the healthcare system must leverage environmentally friendly and energy-efficient methods, including healthcare technologies that use renewable energy, reduce waste, and optimize consumption.

Economic Example:

- **Circular Economy (Sustainable Healthcare):** Companies like **Philips** have already started to integrate circular economy principles into healthcare by focusing on product longevity, recyclability, and reuse. This could be extended into medical equipment, reducing waste and creating a more sustainable healthcare system. By designing healthcare solutions that minimize environmental impact, healthcare delivery could align with global sustainability goals.

- **Energy-efficient Hospitals (Cost Reduction & Sustainability):** Solar-powered or energy-efficient medical facilities could cut operating costs in the long run. Implementing technologies that harness renewable energy sources for medical operations could be subsidized by public health funds, ensuring that sustainability doesn't come at the cost of care.

5. Meritocracy & Value-Based Healthcare

In your meritocratic system, healthcare should reward tangible outcomes. Value-based healthcare, where providers are paid based on patient outcomes rather than services rendered, can be integrated with space exploration as a tool for improving healthcare efficiency and fairness.

Economic Example:

- **Outcome-Based Payment Models (Incentives for High-Quality Care):** Much like economic systems that incentivize results, healthcare systems could pay providers based on patient health outcomes. This might include reducing hospital readmission rates, improving long-term patient health, and utilizing AI to improve patient care efficiency. This shift toward value-based payments would improve the quality of care while reducing inefficiencies and unnecessary procedures.

- **Incentive Structures (Competition & Innovation):** A competitive healthcare system where advancements in technology or treatment lead to greater funding and recognition could spur innovation. For example, companies or countries with the best AI-driven health outcomes might receive funding for further space exploration, thus creating a self-reinforcing cycle of technological advancement, improved healthcare, and financial growth.

6. Global Collaboration & Public-Private Partnerships

The global nature of the healthcare system in this economic model would require international collaboration, public-private partnerships, and the free exchange of knowledge. The vision aligns with the principles of competitive cooperation and international investment to address global challenges.

Economic Example:

- **Public-Private Partnerships (PPPs) for Health Innovation:** Similar to how **the Global Fund** or **GAVI** collaborates across borders to tackle health challenges like pandemics, a new, integrated space-healthcare initiative could pool resources from public, private, and international actors to create sustainable global healthcare solutions. Space agencies could collaborate with healthcare firms to ensure access to cutting-edge medical treatments for all, while also funding space-related innovations that benefit human health.

Conclusion: Healthcare for a Space-faring Civilization

In this forward-thinking economic model, the healthcare system reflects the integration of technology, global cooperation, and sustainability. Through digital health platforms, AI-powered care, resource innovations from space exploration, and a meritocratic framework, the system seeks to ensure that healthcare is not only accessible and sustainable but also incentivizes results and fosters innovation. By addressing economic efficiency, global collaboration, and technological progress, the healthcare system would serve as a cornerstone of the future economy, ensuring both the survival and thriving of humanity in the face of new challenges.

Chapter 12: Making Money in Space. The Space Industry

Making money in space is a rapidly growing field with a wide range of opportunities emerging as technology advances and the cost of space exploration decreases. Here are some ways to profit from space exploration, backed by examples of current and future ventures:

1. Satellite Services

One of the most lucrative ways to make money in space is by offering satellite-based services. These services are used in communications, weather forecasting, global positioning systems (GPS), and Earth observation.

Economic Examples:

- **Satellite Internet (Starlink by SpaceX):** SpaceX's Starlink project aims to provide internet access to underserved regions worldwide by deploying thousands of low Earth orbit (LEO) satellites. This service is already generating significant revenue and is projected to grow as global demand for broadband increases.

- **Earth Observation (Planet Labs):** Companies like Planet Labs, which deploy fleets of small satellites to capture images of Earth, provide valuable data for industries like agriculture, forestry, insurance, and urban planning. These data sets are sold to clients who use them for monitoring crops, predicting weather patterns, and mapping urban growth.

2. Space Mining

The concept of extracting resources from asteroids or other celestial bodies is considered one of the most exciting opportunities for making money in space. These resources could include metals like platinum, gold, or rare minerals, and even water, which is essential for life support on long-term space missions.

Economic Examples:

- **Planetary Resources (now part of ConsenSys):** Planetary Resources aimed to mine asteroids for precious metals. While the company didn't fully develop its mining operations, the idea of mining asteroids for rare materials still holds immense potential.

- **Deep Space Industries:** Another company exploring asteroid mining, with a vision of harvesting water from asteroids to create fuel for spacecraft (this is also seen as a way to create a self-sustaining space economy by "fueling up" in space).

3. Space Tourism

While still in its infancy, space tourism is quickly becoming a potential billion-dollar industry. Companies are working to make space travel accessible to private citizens, offering experiences ranging from suborbital flights to longer stays on space stations.

Economic Examples:

- **Blue Origin (New Shepard):** Founded by Jeff Bezos, Blue Origin is working on suborbital space tourism with plans to take paying customers on short trips to space. These flights have a high price tag (hundreds of thousands of dollars per ticket), but the growing demand could make space tourism a mainstream industry.

- **Virgin Galactic (SpaceShipTwo):** Richard Branson's company aims to take paying customers on suborbital flights for an experience of weightlessness and views of Earth from space. Although these flights are expensive, there's potential for mass market growth as prices decrease over time.

4. Space Manufacturing

Manufacturing in space, particularly in microgravity environments, offers opportunities to create products that cannot be made on Earth, such as unique materials or medical innovations.

Economic Examples:

- **Made in Space:** This company aims to manufacture products in space using 3D printing. They've already created a 3D printer for the International Space Station (ISS) and are exploring the production of advanced materials and components that would be difficult or impossible to make on Earth due to gravity.

- **Orbital Assembly Corporation:** This company is working on building commercial space stations and manufacturing platforms in orbit, where materials and goods could be produced with unique properties thanks to the lack of gravity.

5. Space Infrastructure and Real Estate

In the long run, space infrastructure—like habitats, space stations, and lunar bases—will become vital to sustaining human life and conducting research in space. This could create a space real estate market for construction, leasing, and maintaining such properties.

Economic Examples:

- **Bigelow Aerospace:** Bigelow is developing inflatable habitats that could serve as space stations or temporary homes for astronauts and tourists. These structures could eventually form part of a larger, sustainable space infrastructure.

- **Lunar Real Estate:** As countries like China, the U.S., and private entities explore plans for a lunar base, early pioneers in space construction could sell or lease lunar land, creating a new frontier for real estate and property development.

6. Space-Based Solar Power

The idea of collecting solar energy in space and transmitting it to Earth could revolutionize energy production. Space-based solar power involves placing solar panels in orbit, where the sun shines continuously, and beaming that energy down to Earth.

Economic Example:

- **Solar Power Satellites:** Research institutions and private companies are working to develop space-based solar power systems. Once developed, this system could provide clean, limitless energy to Earth. A space-based solar power system would

potentially have huge economic benefits, as
it could significantly reduce dependence on
fossil fuels.

7. Data & Communication Infrastructure

As space exploration and the use of satellites
increases, so does the demand for data transmission
and communication services. Companies can
provide communication infrastructure to space-
based systems, from satellites to space stations.

Economic Examples:

- **OneWeb:** A company aiming to launch
  thousands of low-orbit satellites to provide
  global internet coverage. They plan to
  generate revenue by offering broadband to
  underserved areas, positioning themselves as
  a significant player in global
  communication.

- **SES Networks:** SES provides satellite
  connectivity to various sectors including
  telecommunications, enterprise, and
  government. As more space-based systems
  come online, the demand for robust
  communication services will increase.

8. Government Contracts and Military Applications

Government contracts, especially with space
agencies like NASA or the European Space Agency
(ESA), are an established way to make money in
space. Additionally, military applications in
space—such as satellite reconnaissance, defense
systems, and space weapons—have the potential to
bring in substantial revenue.

Economic Example:

- **SpaceX and NASA:** SpaceX has won multiple contracts with NASA for cargo and crew transport to the ISS. Their reusable rockets have driven down the cost of space transportation, opening doors for further contracts with both governmental and private sectors.

- **Military Satellites & Space Defense:** Many defense contractors are involved in space projects, from developing spy satellites to space-based missile defense systems. The military's reliance on space for surveillance, communications, and defense is expected to grow, generating ongoing revenue.

9. Space Research & Development

Investing in and conducting scientific research in space, whether in biotechnology, physics, or material sciences, can lead to commercialized breakthroughs that generate profits.

Economic Examples:

- **Space Biotech:** Companies like **Space Tango** are researching how the microgravity environment of space affects biological systems, with potential applications in medicine, agriculture, and more. For example, space research could unlock new drug treatments or agricultural methods.

- **Microgravity Research:** Companies can partner with NASA or other space agencies to conduct experiments in space that result in the development of new technologies that can be patented and commercialized.

10. Space Travel Logistics & Spaceports

As space travel becomes more common, infrastructure for rocket launches, landings, and storage will become essential. Spaceports, ground-based systems for space vehicle preparation, and cargo logistics are becoming key components of space economies.

Economic Example:

- **Virgin Orbit & Rocket Lab:** These companies provide satellite launch services using smaller, more flexible launch vehicles. The ability to offer on-demand, smaller launches is expected to be a significant market in the coming decades.

- **Spaceports:** As demand for space launches grows, building spaceports and providing logistics for travel to and from space will become a significant business opportunity.

Conclusion: The Future of Space Profits

Space offers vast potential for wealth generation, spanning multiple industries, from satellite services to space mining and tourism. The key to success in making money in space lies in identifying niche markets, leveraging technological advancements, and tapping into new business models that emerge as space exploration becomes more routine. With lower launch costs and increasing private-sector involvement, space is no longer just for government agencies or large aerospace companies—it's an open frontier for entrepreneurship, innovation, and wealth creation.

Let's dive even deeper into the emerging opportunities and more detailed ways to make money in space. As the commercial space industry continues to grow, we are starting to see a convergence of sectors that will enable innovative business models. Here are further insights, exploring advanced and potential avenues for wealth generation in space, with economic examples, projections, and the future landscape:

1. Advanced Space Manufacturing

Manufacturing in space opens a whole new world of possibilities, where the unique properties of microgravity can be leveraged to create high-quality products that are impossible or too expensive to produce on Earth. This area has the potential to not only support human expansion in space but also lead to groundbreaking innovations for Earth.

Detailed Examples and Future Potential:

- **3D Printing in Space (Made in Space, SpaceFab):** 3D printing in space offers unique opportunities for producing parts for satellites, spacecraft, and space stations. These products could be manufactured on demand, reducing the need for costly transport of materials from Earth. **Made in Space** has already sent 3D printers to the ISS to create tools and parts. In the future, this could evolve into large-scale space factories producing spacecraft components or even entire structures that would be used for colonies on the Moon or Mars.

- **Advanced Materials:** Manufacturing specialized materials like fiber optics, pharmaceuticals, or new alloys that require zero gravity or low gravity environments for optimal creation. For instance, **ZBLAN**, a glass material made in microgravity, has been shown to have better properties when produced in space compared to on Earth, with significant applications in telecommunications, lasers, and sensors. Space manufacturing could develop materials and products with high demand on Earth, creating a space-based production ecosystem.

Economic Impact: As space-based manufacturing becomes more advanced, businesses that can develop, maintain, and operate space factories could profit from selling high-value, specialized materials. This could revolutionize industries from electronics to medical technologies.

2. Lunar Economy & Resources

The Moon could serve as a launchpad for humanity's further exploration of space, and its resources offer exciting business opportunities. With several countries planning missions to establish a permanent presence on the Moon, there are numerous potential markets that could emerge.

Detailed Examples and Future Potential:

- **Helium-3 Mining:** One of the most intriguing economic possibilities for lunar resource extraction is helium-3, a rare isotope that could be used in nuclear fusion. If fusion power becomes feasible, helium-3 could be a valuable resource. The Moon is considered a major source of helium-3, and mining operations could be lucrative for businesses that set up extraction and transport systems.

- **Lunar Water Extraction:** Water on the Moon, especially from the permanently shadowed craters at the poles, could be converted into hydrogen and oxygen for fuel (liquid hydrogen and oxygen are commonly used in rocket fuel). Extracting water to create a "fuel station" on the Moon for spacecraft traveling deeper into the solar system would be a key business for long-term space exploration.

- **Lunar Construction and Real Estate:** As NASA and private companies such as **SpaceX** plan for lunar bases, companies specializing in construction materials, habitats, and space logistics could capitalize on lunar real estate. Space developers could build lunar habitats or mining operations and lease these facilities to space agencies or private organizations, creating a thriving lunar economy.

Economic Impact: Lunar resources, such as helium-3 and water, could provide the foundation for fueling space missions beyond the Moon, including to Mars. Companies could profit by pioneering resource extraction and supplying critical materials for future missions, while also providing construction services for space habitats.

3. Asteroid Mining – A Multi-Trillion Dollar Industry

Asteroids are rich in precious metals like platinum, gold, and rare Earth metals, as well as water ice that can be turned into fuel for spacecraft. With advances in robotics, AI, and propulsion technology, asteroid mining is becoming a more feasible business model, and several companies are already targeting this market.

Detailed Examples and Future Potential:

- **Planetary Resources & Deep Space Industries:** These companies have been working on asteroid mining technologies. For instance, asteroid **241 Germania** is thought to contain billions of dollars' worth of precious metals, such as platinum and nickel. This could be mined and sent back to Earth, where prices for these materials are high, or used to supply future space exploration projects.

- **In-Situ Resource Utilization (ISRU):** Rather than transporting materials back to Earth, some space companies focus on using asteroid materials to support further space missions. For example, companies could use metals from asteroids to create spacecraft parts, or water from asteroids to refuel vehicles in space.

Economic Impact: Asteroid mining is projected to have massive long-term economic benefits, not just from the raw materials that could be extracted but also in facilitating more cost-efficient space missions. If successful, asteroid mining could be a multi-trillion-dollar industry, driving significant growth in the space economy.

4. Space Debris Management and Recycling

As humanity continues to deploy satellites and spacecraft, the issue of space debris becomes increasingly critical. Companies that can innovate in space debris removal, management, or recycling will be essential to maintaining a sustainable space environment.

Detailed Examples and Future Potential:

- **Debris Removal Technologies (Astroscale, ClearSpace):** Companies like **Astroscale** are developing spacecraft that can actively remove space debris using robotic arms, nets, and even harpoons. Another company, **ClearSpace**, has been working on missions to clean up debris from low Earth orbit (LEO), including old satellites and rocket parts. A growing market for debris removal services is expected as more satellites are launched, with some projections suggesting billions in revenue.

- **Space Waste Recycling:** Recycling in space could involve the reprocessing of decommissioned satellites or space station parts into usable materials for new spacecraft or habitats. SpaceX, for example, could take old Falcon 9 rockets and recycle them into materials for new spacecraft or space infrastructure. The idea of a "circular economy" in space is gaining attention.

Economic Impact: Managing space debris is critical for the longevity of satellite systems and human activity in space. Companies that provide debris removal services or recycling technologies could secure government contracts, as well as sell these technologies to commercial space operators, making debris management a highly profitable sector.

---

5. Space-Based Solar Power (SBSP)

Space-based solar power (SBSP) could revolutionize how we generate and distribute energy on Earth. By placing solar panels in orbit, we could capture sunlight 24/7, without the interference of weather or nighttime. This could provide clean, renewable energy at a scale that is not possible with ground-based solar power.

Detailed Examples and Future Potential:

- **SBSP Prototypes (Space Solar Power Initiative):** NASA and companies like **Solaren** have been exploring the concept of SBSP for years. The idea is to use large arrays of solar panels in orbit to capture sunlight and convert it into microwave energy, which can be transmitted to Earth via a beam. Once fully operational, space-based solar power could provide a constant and sustainable energy source for the planet.

- **Power-to-Earth Systems:** Companies that can create power-to-Earth systems would be able to generate and sell electricity to energy grids, potentially making billions. If space-based solar energy becomes economically viable, it could reduce humanity's dependence on fossil fuels and solve energy scarcity issues in the developing world.

Economic Impact: SBSP could be a breakthrough in the global energy market, with the potential to create a new trillion-dollar industry in energy generation and transmission. It also aligns perfectly with sustainability goals, providing endless, clean energy from space.

---

6. Space Education, Training, and Research

As space becomes increasingly commercialized, there will be an explosion in demand for talent, education, and research in the space sector. Companies offering educational programs, vocational training, or research services related to space exploration can capitalize on this demand.

Detailed Examples and Future Potential:

- **Space Universities and Training Centers:** As the space economy expands, universities like **The International Space University** or space-focused online programs will see increasing demand for new talent in engineering, robotics, and space law. Companies offering specialized certifications or technical training for space engineers, scientists, and astronauts could have high growth potential.

- **Space Research Institutes:** Research in space technology, astrophysics, and planetary science can be monetized by offering consultancy services or by partnering with private companies for joint research projects. Many private companies will need specialized knowledge to overcome the technological challenges of space exploration, opening a lucrative market for research institutes.

Economic Impact: The increasing demand for space-related education and research will generate substantial revenue for educational institutions, research centers, and consultancy firms. This, in turn, will feed into the growing space workforce, enhancing innovation and accelerating the development of new technologies.

Conclusion: The Future of Space Business

As the commercialization of space accelerates, the potential to make money in space grows exponentially. In addition to industries like satellite communications and space tourism, emerging fields such as asteroid mining, space manufacturing, and space-based energy generation could generate trillions of dollars in economic activity over the next several decades. Space will become a vast economic playground, with opportunities for companies, investors, and governments to profit through resource extraction, infrastructure development, and new technologies that support humanity's exploration of the cosmos.

To make money in space, it's crucial to focus on innovation, long-term sustainability, and the integration of technologies that support both the commercial and scientific aspects of space exploration. The businesses that emerge and thrive in this frontier will shape the future of humanity's relationship with space, creating a new era of wealth, progress, and possibility.

Let's explore even deeper, introducing unique concepts and original economic ideas for making money in space, looking beyond conventional approaches. As the boundaries of space exploration and commercial space endeavors expand, innovative economic opportunities are beginning to take shape. Here are new, original ways to profit from space, along with future scenarios that push the envelope of current thinking:

1. Space-Linked Artificial Intelligence Networks

The future of space will not just rely on satellites and human ingenuity but also on advanced artificial intelligence (AI) systems that manage space-based infrastructure, optimize space resource usage, and automate space exploration and production. Space-linked AI networks would act as the brain behind space logistics, satellites, space stations, and even lunar or Martian colonies.

Original Concept:

- **AI-Managed Resource Allocation:** Imagine AI systems that can dynamically control space assets such as satellites, mining operations, and space manufacturing facilities. These AI systems would predict space weather, adjust communication schedules, and ensure efficient usage of space resources (e.g., solar energy or water from asteroids). Through these networks, companies could optimize satellite constellation usage, boosting performance and reducing redundancy. Moreover, as AI in space increases, entire space-based economies could run autonomously—leading to a new wave of services for Earth-bound markets such as AI-managed cloud computing, big data storage, and even deep space data mining.

- **Automated Space Colonies:** Beyond AI operating satellites, you could have entire off-world colonies run with minimal human intervention. AI would manage everything from life-support systems to energy distribution, resource extraction, and health monitoring. A new economy could emerge in which humans become less involved in day-to-day operations but profit from automated technologies that run in space. The AI infrastructure itself could be licensed or sold to space-faring entities, creating a new industry of AI tech specifically for space.

Economic Impact: A space-linked AI ecosystem would create a market for AI-driven satellite services, space station management, and interplanetary automation. Companies providing AI tech, as well as AI-driven space infrastructure companies, could dominate the space economy, adding trillions in value.

2. Space-Based Data Centers (Data Mining & Storage)

Data is becoming one of the most valuable commodities on Earth. Space offers vast opportunities for new types of data storage and computational capabilities—free from the constraints of Earth-based infrastructure, such as the power grid and land use.

Original Concept:

- **Zero-Gravity Data Centers:** In space, data centers could operate in zero-gravity, maximizing server capacity and reducing heat generation due to the natural cooling properties of space. The unique environment could allow for much denser and energy-efficient computing, as well as higher data throughput. These centers could house not just basic cloud storage but also advanced computing systems for AI, machine learning, and scientific simulations.

- **Space Data Mining:** Companies could launch space data mining ventures where data collected from satellites, planetary exploration missions, and space telescopes is processed and analyzed in space-based data centers. This could include deep space observation data (such as from the James Webb Space Telescope) or the vast amounts of data captured by Earth-observing satellites. By processing the data in orbit, companies could send actionable insights back to Earth, saving time and bandwidth while also offering high-value, real-time space data analytics services to industries like climate science, finance, and global security.

Economic Impact: Space-based data centers could become the next big thing for companies like Amazon Web Services (AWS) or Google Cloud, with an entirely new frontier of data storage and processing in orbit. This would generate significant revenue from high-performance computing, real-time analytics, and data mining services. As demand for data grows, these data centers will become integral to our digital infrastructure.

3. Bio-Dome Real Estate: Space-Based Habitats for Earth & Mars

Space habitats and bio-domes on celestial bodies, such as Mars or even asteroids, can become the next frontier for not just research but high-value real estate.

Original Concept:

- **Lunar & Mars Property Development:** Imagine developing a high-end, luxury living and working space for wealthy clients, researchers, or government agencies on the Moon or Mars. Bio-dome habitats could be designed to host families, research teams, or tourists. These environments would offer self-sustaining ecosystems with air, water, and food supplies. Space-based real estate could come with premium services such as space view windows, advanced artificial gravity systems, and 3D-printed homes using local materials (like lunar regolith or Martian dirt).

- **Space Theme Parks & Recreation:** Just as luxury real estate developers on Earth create vacation homes, the same could happen in space. With space tourism growing, there could be recreational zones or hotels on the Moon or Mars for tourists seeking to experience life in space. But these won't just be simple accommodations. Think of underwater hotels on Earth, but in space: zero-gravity environments, long-term stays for high-net-worth individuals, and exploration experiences (like ice-cave tours on Mars or lunar surface expeditions).

Economic Impact: Space-based real estate, combined with the desire for off-planet living and leisure, could create a massive market for commercial space properties. This could turn into a trillion-dollar industry, with the early adopters of space real estate profiting from the first human settlements in space.

---

4. Interstellar Logistics – The Space Supply Chain

With future missions aimed at not just the Moon or Mars but further destinations in our solar system and beyond, there's a growing need for supply chain logistics in space. The infrastructure that connects various space missions will create a new market for off-world transportation and resource management.

Original Concept:

- **Space Freight Companies:** Launching and operating supply ships that carry everything from raw materials for space stations and lunar colonies to satellites and spacecraft for exploration. These ships would operate between Earth, the Moon, Mars, and eventually outer planets or asteroids, acting as space-based freight companies. Space ports on the Moon, Mars, and orbiting space stations would be the hubs for these interplanetary shipping companies.

- **Interplanetary Fuel Stations:** Much like the oil rigs and refueling stations on Earth, we could establish space-based refueling stations. These would extract or produce fuel (like hydrogen or methane) on the Moon or Mars, and act as refueling points for space vessels making long trips to Jupiter or beyond. Companies could profit by providing fuel to spacecraft traveling between Earth and Mars, or between different regions of the solar system.

Economic Impact: Interstellar logistics could be a multi-billion-dollar industry, as it will play a critical role in the movement of people, supplies, and resources throughout the solar system. These logistics companies will provide the infrastructure that supports space tourism, exploration, and resource extraction, making them an essential part of the space economy.

5. Space-Based Carbon Capture and Environmental Technologies

In the future, space could become an essential part of tackling Earth's environmental challenges. Space-based carbon capture systems and solar-powered environmental technologies could provide solutions to issues like climate change, pollution, and natural resource depletion.

Original Concept:

- **Space Carbon Capture:** A space-based carbon capture system could extract carbon dioxide from Earth's atmosphere and process it in orbit. Large solar-powered arrays in space could use chemical processes to collect and transform CO_2 into useful products like oxygen, methane, or even synthetic fuels. These products could then be sent back to Earth or used to fuel space operations. By capturing excess CO_2 in space, this system could significantly reduce the global impact of climate change.

- **Space-Powered Earth Clean-Up:** Imagine space-based solar panels that could power large-scale environmental clean-up operations on Earth, such as ocean plastic collection or wildfire suppression. These systems could draw energy from space to carry out global missions to tackle pressing environmental issues.

Economic Impact: Space-based solutions for environmental challenges would tap into the growing sustainability market. By offering products and services that directly address climate change and environmental degradation, companies involved in space-powered environmental technologies could not only generate substantial revenue but also secure long-term government contracts and global partnerships focused on environmental restoration.

---

6. Space-Backed Digital Assets & Space-NFTs

Digital assets, including cryptocurrencies and NFTs (non-fungible tokens), have taken the Earth by storm. What if space could provide a unique, scalable solution for space-backed digital assets and space-related NFTs? These could be tied to real-world space endeavors, like ownership of lunar land, asteroid mining rights, or even virtual land on Mars.

Original Concept:

- **Space-NFTs for Digital Collectibles:**
  Companies could create space-themed
  digital art or memorabilia (such as moon
  surface images, lunar mining rights, or
  historic space mission moments) and sell
  them as NFTs. These unique assets could be
  tied to real space operations—making these
  NFTs valuable in the digital economy.

- **Space-Based Cryptocurrencies:** A
  cryptocurrency could be backed by actual
  space assets (such as asteroid mining rights,
  space station shares, or lunar land). This
  would create a space-backed blockchain that
  could be used to conduct space transactions,
  buy space-based products, or even offer
  investment in space exploration projects.

Economic Impact: Space-backed digital assets like
space-NFTs and space-based cryptocurrencies could
revolutionize the way we view value exchange in
space. The blockchain-powered economy would
allow investors to own fractionalized space assets,
enabling liquidity and the democratization of space
investment.

Conclusion: A New Economic Frontier in Space

As the space economy continues to evolve, these
novel, original approaches to profit in space offer
entirely new ways to tap into this emerging frontier.
The key to success in space business will not only
be technical innovation but also creative and
forward-thinking economic models that combine
current technologies, space exploration, and
sustainability efforts. The potential to create truly
new industries—spanning from space data services

to off-world real estate, interstellar logistics, and even digital space assets—will define the next generation of wealth creation, not just on Earth, but across the cosmos.

Mining in space offers a vast array of resources that are either scarce or not readily available on Earth. These materials are crucial for supporting long-term human activities in space, as well as advancing various industries on Earth. Here's an in-depth look at the types of materials that could be mined in space:

1. Precious Metals (Gold, Platinum, Palladium)

Many asteroids in our solar system contain high concentrations of precious metals, which are extremely rare on Earth and often difficult to mine. Some asteroids are rich in platinum-group metals (PGMs) like platinum, palladium, and rhodium, which are essential in electronics, automotive catalysts, and various high-tech industries.

- **Example: Asteroid 241 Germania** is believed to have large amounts of platinum-group metals, making it a prime target for asteroid mining.

- **Economic Value:** These metals are valuable both on Earth and in space, where they could be used for constructing spacecraft, space stations, or even in creating specialized electronics for space missions.

2. Rare Earth Elements (REEs)

Rare Earth Elements (REEs) are critical for producing electronics, renewable energy technologies (such as wind turbines and solar panels), and electric vehicle batteries. On Earth, these elements are often difficult and expensive to extract, but in space, certain asteroids may contain high concentrations of REEs.

- **Example: Asteroids like 52 Europa** are thought to contain large quantities of REEs, such as neodymium and dysprosium, which are essential in manufacturing magnets and electronics.

- **Economic Value:** Mining REEs in space could alleviate supply chain concerns on Earth and provide these materials for advanced manufacturing, space propulsion systems, and even quantum computing.

3. Water (H2O)

Water in space is not just a critical resource for human survival in space but also an essential component for producing fuel and supporting life-support systems. Water ice is believed to be abundant on certain asteroids, the Moon, and especially on Mars, where it can be used for both life support and rocket fuel.

- **Example: The Moon has large quantities of water ice** in permanently shadowed craters at its poles, where the temperature is so low that ice has remained stable for billions of years.

- **Economic Value:** Water can be converted into oxygen (O2) for breathable air, hydrogen (H2) for rocket fuel (via electrolysis), and used for agricultural purposes on space stations or lunar/Martian colonies. Water mining could support a self-sustaining human presence in space.

4. Helium-3 (He-3)

Helium-3 is a rare isotope of helium that has gained attention due to its potential use in nuclear fusion. Unlike conventional nuclear fission, fusion using helium-3 could provide a nearly limitless and clean energy source. Helium-3 is thought to be abundant on the Moon, particularly in the lunar regolith (soil), and mining it could open the door to clean energy both on Earth and in space.

- **Example: The Moon's regolith** contains trace amounts of helium-3, which could be extracted and used in future fusion reactors.

- **Economic Value:** The development of nuclear fusion energy using helium-3 would be revolutionary, offering a clean, almost limitless energy source for Earth and space colonies. The market for helium-3 could be worth trillions, making it one of the most sought-after resources for space mining.

5. Iron, Nickel, and Cobalt

Common metals like iron, nickel, and cobalt are essential for building infrastructure on Earth and in space. These metals are needed for creating spacecraft, tools, space stations, and other technologies. Certain asteroids contain large quantities of these metals, which could be mined and used either for space-based construction or shipped back to Earth.

- **Example: Asteroids like 243 Ida and 243 Matilda** contain significant amounts of iron, nickel, and cobalt, making them attractive targets for mining.

- **Economic Value:** These metals can be used in the construction of spacecraft, rovers, habitats, and other infrastructure in space. Mining these materials in space could reduce the need to launch heavy materials from Earth, lowering costs and making space exploration and colonization more feasible.

6. Silicon

Silicon is a fundamental material for electronics and solar panels. In space, it is crucial for creating solar arrays, which are used to power satellites and space stations. Asteroids and the Moon could serve as a source of silicon, which could be mined and used to manufacture solar panels and other space technologies.

- **Example: The asteroid 243 Ida** contains minerals rich in silicon.

- **Economic Value:** The ability to mine silicon in space could support the construction of solar panels for energy generation in space and on Earth. Space-based solar power systems could become more cost-effective if silicon is sourced directly from space.

7. Carbon

Carbon-based materials are used extensively in the aerospace industry, from carbon composites used in spacecraft construction to carbon-based fuels. In space, carbon could be mined from asteroids or other celestial bodies in the form of carbonaceous chondrites—asteroids that are rich in organic compounds and carbon.

- **Example: Carbon-rich asteroids like 162173 Ryugu** are considered potential sources of valuable carbon compounds.

- **Economic Value:** Carbon could be converted into carbon nanotubes or graphene, which have applications in lightweight, high-strength materials for space infrastructure, electronics, and energy storage.

8. Magnesium and Aluminum

Magnesium and aluminum are lightweight metals that are widely used in aerospace construction due to their strength-to-weight ratio. These metals could be mined from asteroids or the Moon and used for building spacecraft, habitats, and other infrastructure.

- **Example: The asteroid 243 Ida** also contains aluminum and magnesium-rich minerals that could be extracted for use in space projects.

- **Economic Value:** These metals would be essential for constructing long-term space stations, rovers, and habitats on the Moon, Mars, or other celestial bodies, significantly reducing reliance on Earth-based metal production.

9. Sulfur

Sulfur is an essential component for various industrial processes, including the production of fertilizers, chemicals, and pharmaceuticals. Some asteroids, as well as celestial bodies like Venus, have sulfur in their regolith or atmosphere, making them potential targets for mining.

- **Example: Asteroids and moons like Io (Jupiter's moon) have high sulfur content, which could be mined and processed in space.

- **Economic Value:** Sulfur could be used for industrial processes in space, including the production of chemicals and as a potential feedstock for manufacturing fuel or other useful compounds.

10. Ammonia

Ammonia is crucial for the production of fertilizers and could be used as a propellant in space missions. Certain asteroids and planetary bodies like Mars might have ammonia in their composition.

- **Example: The surface of Mars is believed to have ammonia in its soil, which could be mined for use in space agriculture or as a resource for propellants.

- **Economic Value:** Mining ammonia from space could help produce food for space colonies and also provide fuel for rockets or space vehicles, making it a valuable resource for long-term space missions.

11. Titanium and Zirconium

Titanium is used extensively in aerospace applications due to its strength and resistance to corrosion. It could be found in the regolith of the Moon or in asteroid material. Similarly, zirconium is used in spacecraft propulsion and as a heat-resistant material in reactors and other equipment.

- **Example: Asteroids such as 243 Ida and 253 Mathilde** have been found to contain significant concentrations of titanium and zirconium.

- **Economic Value:** These metals would be key to building resilient space infrastructure and could be used in spacecraft, habitats, and high-performance technologies.

Space Mining: A New Frontier for Sustainability and Profit

As technology continues to improve and space exploration becomes more feasible, the mining of these materials will play an essential role in supporting both Earth's economy and the burgeoning space economy. Mining in space not only offers the potential for valuable resources but also enables the establishment of sustainable, long-term human presence beyond Earth.

The key challenges, such as the development of mining technology, transportation systems, and legal frameworks for resource ownership, will need to be addressed as the industry matures. However, the vast wealth of untapped resources in space represents one of the most exciting frontiers for human ingenuity and economic growth in the 21st century.

Let's dive even further into space resources that could be mined, but this time focusing on even more unique and lesser-known materials. These new examples are not only fascinating but could potentially play pivotal roles in the future of space exploration and Earth industries. By exploring unconventional materials that could be found or produced in space, we can truly stretch the imagination of what a space economy might look like.

1. Amorphous Metals (Bulk Metallic Glasses)

Amorphous metals, or Bulk Metallic Glasses (BMGs), are unique metallic alloys that lack a crystalline structure. These materials are incredibly strong, resistant to corrosion, and highly durable, making them perfect for use in harsh environments like space. Due to their unique atomic structure, BMGs also have superior elastic properties, meaning they can withstand extreme forces without breaking.

- **Example:** Asteroids with high concentrations of silicon and metals like nickel, iron, or cobalt could be refined into BMGs. These materials may be abundant in bodies that have undergone slow cooling and crystallization over millions of years.

- **Economic Value:** In space construction, these amorphous metals could be used for everything from spacecraft hulls to habitat frames, offering durability and efficiency. Their ability to withstand radiation and micrometeorite impacts makes them ideal for long-term space missions and infrastructure on the Moon or Mars.

2. Lunar Regolith for 3D Printing (In-Situ Resource Utilization)

The Moon's surface, known as lunar regolith, is full of untapped resources, including oxygen, metals, and silicates. By using advanced 3D printing technologies, these materials could be processed and converted into building blocks for habitats, infrastructure, and even tools.

- **Example:** Lunar regolith contains abundant amounts of aluminum, silicon, iron, calcium, magnesium, and oxygen, which can be combined with advanced processing technologies to create concrete-like materials, useful for constructing lunar bases or even producing 3D-printed machinery.

- **Economic Value:** Using lunar regolith for construction would be essential for sustainable living on the Moon or Mars. The ability to "print" buildings and structures directly from lunar resources would drastically reduce the costs of bringing construction materials from Earth, and could lead to the creation of entire colonies on the Moon with minimal need for Earth-based supplies.

---

3. Palladium, Rhodium, and Iridium for Catalysis

The precious metals palladium, rhodium, and iridium, known for their catalytic properties, are used in numerous high-tech applications on Earth, including hydrogen fuel production, automotive catalytic converters, and organic synthesis in chemical industries. These metals are also believed to be abundant in certain asteroids.

- **Example:** Asteroids rich in these metals, like those from the *M-type* category (metallic asteroids), can be sources for palladium, rhodium, and iridium. These asteroids have a high concentration of metals, particularly those used in catalytic processes.

- **Economic Value:** Mining these metals would be crucial for space-based manufacturing, especially in developing clean energy solutions (e.g., hydrogen fuel cells for space missions) and advanced technology on Earth. The demand for these metals could increase dramatically as we shift toward clean energy, making their extraction a potentially lucrative business in space.

4. Tungsten (W) and Rhenium (Re) for High-Temperature Applications

Tungsten and rhenium are incredibly heat-resistant metals, with high melting points, making them essential in space exploration, particularly in propulsion systems, rocket nozzles, and aerospace components that are exposed to extreme heat.

- **Example:** Asteroids that are rich in metals like iron and nickel also contain trace amounts of tungsten and rhenium. The asteroid *16 Psyche*, for instance, is thought to contain high levels of iron and could potentially be a source for these heat-resistant metals.

- **Economic Value:** These metals could be key in advancing space travel and exploration. Their ability to withstand extreme temperatures without degrading makes them ideal for the construction of space propulsion systems, heat shields for re-entry, and parts of space mining equipment. As space exploration progresses, especially with interplanetary travel, demand for these metals will rise significantly.

---

5. Carbon Nanotubes (CNTs) and Graphene

Carbon nanotubes and graphene are materials with extraordinary properties—exceptional strength, lightness, and electrical conductivity. These materials are expected to play a significant role in future technological innovations on Earth, from advanced electronics to space exploration. Both materials can be synthesized in space, where their properties could be enhanced due to the low gravity and unique conditions.

- **Example:** Carbon-rich asteroids, such as *162173 Ryugu*, are known to contain large amounts of organic compounds and carbon, which can be processed to create carbon nanotubes or graphene. Additionally, carbon could be harvested from the carbonaceous chondrites of these asteroids.

- **Economic Value:** The demand for CNTs and graphene is expected to soar in the fields of energy storage, electronics, construction, and even medical technology. Space mining operations could provide these high-demand materials for both space-based infrastructure and advanced manufacturing back on Earth. Their use in lightweight, high-strength components for spacecraft, solar panels, or energy storage systems could revolutionize space travel and technology.

6. Sodium and Potassium for Electrolytes in Batteries

Sodium and potassium are critical elements in the development of next-generation batteries, particularly in energy storage systems for both terrestrial and space applications. Space-based sources of these elements could be highly beneficial, as they are abundant in various celestial bodies and could support energy solutions for both space colonies and Earth.

- **Example:** Asteroids containing sodium and potassium salts could be mined for use in manufacturing energy storage systems. In particular, the asteroid *243 Ida* is believed to contain a high percentage of sodium and potassium-rich compounds.

- **Economic Value:** By extracting these elements for advanced battery technologies (such as sodium-ion or potassium-ion batteries), space mining could help address the growing demand for energy storage solutions on Earth. These types of batteries are seen as a viable alternative to lithium-ion batteries, especially in regions with limited lithium resources.

7. Zinc and Copper for Electrical Infrastructure

Zinc and copper are essential for electrical infrastructure, wiring, and electronic devices. These metals are critical to building and powering spacecraft, as well as maintaining electrical systems in space colonies or stations.

- **Example:** Zinc and copper can be found in some asteroids with metallic compositions. For example, the asteroid *243 Ida* contains significant amounts of both metals. Mining these metals from space would allow for the development of reliable electrical infrastructure in space.

- **Economic Value:** Copper and zinc are already highly valuable on Earth, and their applications in space infrastructure—such as wiring, electrical grids, and electronic components—could be even more critical. Mining these materials in space would allow for self-sustaining colonies that are less reliant on Earth-based supply chains, while also providing an economic market for these metals on Earth.

8. Magnesium-Lithium Alloys for Spacecraft Construction

Magnesium-lithium alloys are light, strong, and resistant to corrosion, making them ideal for spacecraft construction. These alloys could be utilized for both structural and thermal management applications in spacecraft and space habitats.

- **Example:** Magnesium and lithium are both abundant in certain asteroids. Asteroids that are rich in magnesium silicates, such as *243 Ida*, could also contain significant quantities of lithium, which can be refined into magnesium-lithium alloys.

- **Economic Value:** The demand for these lightweight and high-strength materials will increase as space exploration progresses. These alloys would play a vital role in building efficient spacecraft that require lightweight but durable construction materials to withstand the harsh conditions of space travel, while also improving fuel efficiency for space missions.

9. Silicon Carbide (SiC) for Semiconductor Industry

Silicon carbide (SiC) is a semiconductor material that is used in electronics and power systems due to its superior heat tolerance, high voltage resistance, and electrical efficiency. Its potential applications in power transmission and high-performance electronics are highly sought after, especially in space technologies.

- **Example:** Asteroids rich in carbon (such as carbonaceous asteroids) and silicon compounds could yield silicon carbide. Mining these materials could involve the synthesis of SiC in space laboratories that take advantage of the low-gravity environment, which might increase the efficiency of SiC crystals.

- **Economic Value:** The production of silicon carbide semiconductors in space could lead to significant technological advancements in electronics and power systems, both in space and on Earth. With the growing demand for high-performance electronic devices, power electronics, and electric vehicles, space-based silicon carbide could become a key market in the global tech industry.

10. Sulfur and Phosphorus for Agricultural Expansion

Sulfur and phosphorus are essential elements for the growth of plants, and both are necessary for fertilizers. In space, they could be harvested from asteroids or moons like *Io*, one of Jupiter's moons, which is rich in sulfur compounds. These materials would be crucial for supporting space-based agriculture, ensuring food sustainability for future space colonies.

- **Example:** Moons like *Io* have extensive sulfur-rich deposits, which could be used to produce fertilizers for agricultural use in space. Phosphorus could also be mined from asteroids and moons rich in phosphates.

- **Economic Value:** These materials could be integral for sustaining long-term human habitats in space by supporting agricultural efforts. Additionally, their extraction and use in space could pave the way for producing food more efficiently in off-world colonies, thus reducing the need for Earth-based supplies and making space colonization more self-sufficient.

Conclusion: Expanding the Space Economy

As we envision the future of space exploration, the range of materials available for mining grows increasingly diverse and valuable. From rare earth elements to high-tech semiconductors, advanced alloys, and essential resources for sustainable living, the potential for space mining is vast. The economic benefits of mining these materials could not only drive the growth of space-based industries but also transform Earth's technology landscape, offering new solutions for energy, manufacturing, and sustainability. By venturing into these uncharted territories, humanity stands to unlock new markets and technologies, ensuring a future where space is not just explored, but truly inhabited and harnessed for progress. And that is the Modern Economy.

Chapter 13: Sanitation and Waste Disposal

Designing a sanitation and waste disposal system for a space economy that includes the mining of rare materials from asteroids and celestial bodies would be crucial to ensure sustainability and efficiency in space habitats and operations. The system must account for the unique challenges of space, such as microgravity, limited space, and the need for resource conservation. Here's an innovative, sustainable, and efficient sanitation and waste disposal system designed specifically for a space-based economy:

1. Closed-Loop Waste Management System

Given the limitations of space environments, waste management must be closed-loop, meaning all waste should either be recycled or reused, minimizing the need for external resources. The system would have three primary categories: human waste, organic waste, and inorganic waste (such as metals, plastics, and packaging materials). The closed-loop system would be based on advanced technologies for recycling, resource recovery, and composting.

a. Human Waste Recycling (Biological Waste Processing)

Human waste will be processed using a bio-digestive system that converts organic waste into reusable resources. This process involves microbial digestion of feces, urine, and other organic material to produce essential outputs for the space habitat, such as water and fertilizers.

- **Process:** Microorganisms will break down organic material in an anaerobic chamber, converting the waste into biogas (methane) for energy production and clean water through filtration. The remaining organic slurry can be processed into nutrient-rich compost for use in agriculture (e.g., space farming). The water recovery systems would purify the waste by removing contaminants, making it suitable for reuse in other habitat systems like drinking water or agricultural irrigation.

- **Technology:** Advanced microbial fuel cells (MFCs) can be used to create electricity from the biogas produced during the waste processing. These cells would power essential systems within the habitat.

b. Water Recovery and Filtration Systems

Water is one of the most critical resources in space habitats, and its recycling and filtration will be a central component of the sanitation system. The space station or colony will use advanced filtration systems to purify water from human waste, used water from agricultural processes, and even water extracted from the surrounding environment (e.g., lunar ice or atmospheric moisture).

- **Technologies:** The system would incorporate reverse osmosis, ultraviolet sterilization, and activated carbon filters to ensure that water can be reused for drinking, cooking, cleaning, and agricultural needs.

- **Mining Synergies:** The lunar regolith, which contains oxygen, can be used in conjunction with these water recovery systems to support human life and convert waste water into usable water for various functions.

---

2. Inorganic Waste Processing (Resource Recovery and Recycling)

Inorganic waste, such as materials used in construction, packaging, and tools, must be carefully managed and repurposed to avoid accumulation in space. Space-based mining operations, especially those involving materials like tungsten, copper, or palladium, produce significant waste streams that need to be handled efficiently.

a. 3D Printing of Inorganic Materials

One of the key benefits of space mining is the ability to use extracted materials to create 3D-printed components. Asteroids, moons, and other celestial bodies could provide metals like tungsten, rhenium, and copper, which would be valuable for space infrastructure.

- **Process:** Instead of throwing away scraps of metal, they could be collected and processed for use in 3D printing. Advanced 3D printers capable of utilizing a variety of materials could use recycled metals, plastics, or composites to build infrastructure, machinery, or replacement parts.

- **Technology:** Inorganic waste could be sorted into specific types—metals, plastics, and ceramics—and then recycled into the appropriate raw materials for construction or maintenance of space equipment and habitats.

b. Automated Recycling Bots

To streamline waste management, automated robots equipped with sorting mechanisms can be deployed to separate recyclable materials. These robots would be responsible for breaking down waste into smaller pieces and sorting materials by their properties (metals, plastics, composites, etc.).

- **Technology:** Robots could use artificial intelligence (AI) and machine learning algorithms to optimize the recycling process, ensuring that valuable resources are not lost and are instead directed to the most efficient recycling or repurposing processes.

3. Organic Waste for Agriculture (Closed-Loop Farming)

In a space-based economy, food production is essential for long-term sustainability. Space farming will be required to ensure that colonies are self-sufficient, reducing the reliance on Earth for fresh food supplies. Organic waste will be used as a valuable resource for agriculture, contributing to the closed-loop waste system.

a. Composting and Soil Enrichment

Organic waste, such as plant matter, food scraps, and other biodegradable materials, can be composted and converted into rich, fertile soil for growing crops. The waste will be processed through aerobic digestion, which creates humus—a soil-like material that can improve crop yields.

- **Technology:** Advanced composting chambers will use controlled conditions of temperature, moisture, and airflow to break down organic matter efficiently. The enriched soil can be used in hydroponic or aeroponic farming systems, reducing the need for Earth-based fertilizers and allowing for sustainable food production in space habitats.

- **Mining Synergies:** Space colonies may use minerals like sulfur and phosphorus (mined from asteroids or moons like Io) to enhance the quality of the soil and improve plant growth, providing a complete waste-to-resource loop.

---

4. Microgravity Waste Compaction (Efficient Waste Storage)

Waste storage in microgravity presents unique challenges, as there is no gravity to keep waste in containers. In addition, waste volume must be minimized to conserve space. Waste compaction and vacuum-sealing will be key processes for dealing with non-recyclable waste.

a. Vacuum Sealed Bags

Waste that cannot be recycled or repurposed, such as non-biodegradable materials, will be compacted into vacuum-sealed bags to eliminate excess air and reduce storage volume. These sealed bags would then be securely stored in designated waste management compartments, designed to minimize exposure to the rest of the habitat.

- **Process:** Non-recyclable waste like packaging materials, old electronics, and broken equipment would be compacted and sealed in a way that prevents contamination or leakage. Over time, these materials can either be repurposed or disposed of safely, depending on their content.

b. Waste Compression and Melting

For certain types of materials like plastics or metals, high-pressure compaction followed by melting could allow these waste materials to be reused in space-based manufacturing. Advanced space furnaces could melt down plastic waste to be molded into useful parts or tools, or even be used to create new materials for 3D printing.

---

5. Waste Disposal via Space-Ejection (Safe Disposal of Non-Recyclable Waste)

In cases where waste is truly non-recyclable, it may need to be disposed of by ejecting it into deep space, far away from any active space missions or colonies. However, this process must be tightly controlled to avoid littering space with debris.

- **Process:** After all possible resources have been extracted from the waste, it would be compacted, stored, and ejected via controlled mechanisms. The disposal will occur in a way that ensures no collision with important satellites, space stations, or other celestial bodies.

- **Technology:** Magnetic launchers or ion thrusters could be used to eject waste at high speeds, ensuring it is sent into deep space, effectively removing it from the space economy's ecosystem.

6. Waste-to-Energy Conversion (Power Generation from Waste)

Some of the waste generated from space activities could be converted into energy, contributing to the colony's power needs. Organic waste can be processed through anaerobic digestion to generate biogas, and even some inorganic waste, such as plastics or synthetic materials, can be burned in controlled environments to produce heat and electricity.

- **Process:** Waste-to-energy systems would capture methane gas from organic waste and use it to generate electricity. The remaining solid waste could be burned or thermally processed to create usable heat, which could then be converted into power.

- **Technology:** Thermoelectric generators or other advanced technologies could be integrated into the waste processing systems, providing power for the colony's life support systems, mining operations, or manufacturing processes.

Conclusion: A Self-Sustaining Space Economy

A space economy built around resource extraction, manufacturing, and space habitation will need to incorporate innovative sanitation and waste disposal systems to ensure sustainability. By utilizing advanced technologies like closed-loop waste recycling, waste-to-energy systems, 3D printing, and efficient compaction and storage methods, space colonies and mining operations can ensure that they remain self-sustaining, minimize their environmental impact, and continue to thrive in the harsh conditions of space. The key to success will be maximizing resource recovery, minimizing waste, and reusing as much as possible, creating a truly circular space economy.

Designing a sanitation and waste disposal system in space, particularly with a focus on environmental conservation, requires a deep understanding of both ecological principles and the economic systems that govern resource allocation. In a space-based economy, sustainability and responsible resource use will be at the core of any functional infrastructure, given the finite nature of resources and the unique constraints of space environments. In this in-depth exploration, we will build a system that not only conserves resources and minimizes waste but also incorporates economic principles like efficiency, externalities, and sustainability to ensure long-term viability for both space missions and future space colonies.

Key Environmental Conservation Principles

1. **Closed-Loop Systems:** A space economy will rely heavily on closed-loop systems, where every input (resource) is used efficiently, and every output (waste) is either recycled or repurposed. This principle is rooted in *circular economics*, which emphasizes reducing waste and maximizing resource utilization. Waste is not seen as an externality to be discarded, but as a resource to be reintegrated into the system.

2. **Resource Efficiency and Minimization:** The economic principle of *marginal efficiency of resources* must be applied to

ensure that space resources are not overexploited. The cost of extracting, processing, and transporting materials in space is extraordinarily high, so minimizing unnecessary resource use is essential. This can be achieved through efficient resource recovery and the minimization of waste in every stage of space operations.

3. **Sustainability and Long-Term Value:** The concept of *intergenerational equity* emphasizes the importance of using resources in a way that does not compromise the ability of future generations to meet their own needs. This principle applies in space as much as on Earth, ensuring that any waste management or resource extraction system is designed for long-term sustainability, and that the environmental impact is minimized to avoid degrading the space environment or harming future space missions.

Economic and Environmental Considerations for Space Waste Disposal

1. Waste Prevention and Minimization: Economic Incentives

Before waste disposal even occurs, the system must prioritize waste prevention and minimization. In economic terms, the *opportunity cost* of producing waste in space is high—resources used to create waste could otherwise be used for more productive, value-adding activities. Waste, particularly non-recyclable waste, not only takes up valuable space but also consumes energy and resources to manage.

Preventing waste at the source is essential for sustainability.

- **Design for Durability and Reuse:** Economic efficiency can be achieved by designing materials, equipment, and systems in space that have a long lifespan and can be easily repaired or reused. For instance, spacecraft, habitats, and mining equipment could be built with high-quality, durable materials (such as BMGs or graphene) that reduce wear and tear. This would decrease the need for replacing parts and minimize waste generated by breakdowns.

  - **Example:** In asteroid mining, advanced technologies like autonomous mining robots or 3D printers could be designed with durability in mind, reducing wear-related waste. These robots could be repaired and repurposed, preventing the need for new materials to replace broken components.

- **Design for Resource Recovery:** Much like the concept of "design for disassembly" in Earth-based manufacturing, space systems could be designed for easy resource recovery. By ensuring that components are modular, repairable, and recyclable, waste can be minimized at the end of their life cycle. Economic efficiency would be maximized because the resources spent on extraction, transportation, and processing could be recaptured and reused.

2. Waste-to-Resource Conversion:

For a truly sustainable and environmentally conscious waste management system, *resource recovery* is critical. This concept goes beyond waste recycling, converting waste into valuable materials that can either be reused in space or sent back to Earth for economic gain.

- **Organic Waste for Agricultural Systems:** Space farming systems will rely on biological waste—such as human waste, plant matter, and food scraps—as a resource for growing crops. In economic terms, this is an example of *resource efficiency*—the value of organic waste is maximized by converting it into fertilizers for space agriculture. This eliminates the need to bring agricultural inputs from Earth, reducing both economic costs and environmental impact.

  - **Example:** A bio-digestive system could break down human waste to create biogas for energy and use the nutrient-rich slurry to produce fertilizers for space farming. This ensures that food production is self-sustaining, and organic waste does not accumulate.

- **Inorganic Waste for Manufacturing:** The space economy should focus on using waste for 3D printing or manufacturing new equipment and materials. By incorporating a *closed-loop manufacturing model*, space-based industries can continually reuse scrap materials to create new tools, structures, or machinery, contributing to sustainability. This principle also ties into the concept of *capital preservation*—by continuously recycling valuable metals and plastics, the economic value of these materials is preserved.

- o **Example:** Metals like palladium, rhodium, and iridium—used in catalytic processes—can be recovered from electronic waste and reused for space-based manufacturing or fuel production, reducing the need for mining new resources. Similarly, carbon nanotubes and graphene, when processed from carbon-rich asteroids, can be recycled into new, stronger materials for space infrastructure.

3. Waste-to-Energy: Economic Valuation of Energy Recovery

A key component of an environmentally conscious waste management system is converting waste into energy. In space, the opportunity cost of generating energy is high, as resources must be carefully allocated. Waste-to-energy systems can generate power from non-recyclable or unwanted waste, thus providing energy while reducing landfill accumulation.

- **Waste-to-Energy Systems:** These systems would use heat or chemical processes to convert waste, such as plastics, into usable energy. In space habitats, this energy could power essential systems like life support, manufacturing, and communication networks. From an economic standpoint, *energy efficiency* and *cost minimization* are achieved by extracting value from waste materials instead of relying on external power sources.

- o **Example:** Non-recyclable plastic waste could be converted into electricity using pyrolysis or other thermal processes. This energy could be used to fuel environmental control systems or even assist in powering mining operations on distant asteroids.

- **Methane Recovery for Space Propulsion:** Organic waste, such as food scraps and human waste, can be converted into biogas, specifically methane. This methane could serve as a form of *green energy* for propulsion systems or power generation. By using waste to produce fuel, the economic efficiency of energy generation is increased, reducing reliance on Earth-based fuel sources and minimizing environmental impact.

4. Sustainable Waste Disposal in Space:

Though recycling and recovery are paramount, not all waste can be reused. When waste must be disposed of, it should be done in a way that minimizes environmental harm and avoids creating harmful space debris. The economic principle of *negative externalities*—unintended consequences of an economic activity that affect others—can be applied here to ensure that space waste disposal is done responsibly.

- **Space Waste Disposal Mechanisms:** Non-recyclable waste can be ejected into deep space using controlled methods. The cost of this waste disposal should include not only financial considerations but also the potential long-term environmental costs (e.g., creating more debris in space that could impact future missions). Ensuring that waste disposal activities do not affect critical space infrastructure requires careful planning, with mechanisms in place to ensure that waste is sent into regions of space where it cannot interfere with current or future missions.

- o **Example:** Using magnetic launchers or ion thrusters to propel non-recyclable waste into deep space ensures it does not pose a danger to satellites, space stations, or future space missions. Additionally, environmental monitoring systems will be employed to track the trajectory of discarded waste.

- **Space Debris Mitigation:** Economic models should also account for the *long-term costs* of space debris, which can damage spacecraft and increase mission risks. Mitigating space debris involves building spacecraft and satellites that can safely de-orbit at the end of their life cycle, or that can be repurposed for further use. This practice would also contribute to reducing the environmental footprint of space activities.

Integrating Environmental Economics into Space Waste Management

1. Pricing Externalities: Environmental externalities, such as the cost of pollution or resource depletion, can be priced into space activities. By incorporating the *social cost of carbon* and other environmental impacts into the economics of space-based waste management, space agencies and companies will have a clearer understanding of the true costs of their activities. These costs can be internalized through systems such as carbon taxes or waste disposal fees, which will incentivize the reduction of waste and more efficient resource use.

2. Resource Valuation: The economic principle of *resource valuation* can be applied to determine the true worth of recycling materials or converting waste into energy. By assigning monetary value to waste streams—such as the value of recovered metals, energy produced from waste, or agricultural products grown from organic waste—space-based economies can incentivize the development of waste processing technologies that maximize resource recovery.

3. Cost-Benefit Analysis: To ensure that the sanitation and waste disposal systems are economically viable, rigorous *cost-benefit analysis* should be conducted. This would evaluate the financial costs of waste management, such as the installation and maintenance of recycling and energy recovery technologies, against the benefits, including the value of recovered resources, energy savings, and reduced reliance on Earth-based supplies. Optimizing waste systems based on these analyses will ensure that space missions and colonies remain economically sustainable.

Conclusion: Environmental Conservation and Economic Sustainability in Space

In designing a sanitation and waste disposal system for space, environmental conservation should be a top priority. By applying key economic principles such as closed-loop resource cycles, efficient resource allocation, and minimizing negative externalities, we can create an infrastructure that supports long-term sustainability. This system will ensure that space habitats not only thrive in terms of resource use but do so while minimizing their environmental impact, contributing to a truly sustainable space economy.

Chapter 14: Morals, Values, and Ethics in the Modern Economy

System of Morals, Values, and Ethics for the Vision of Modern Economics:

Th Modern Economic system is rooted in the principles of progress, equality, sustainability, and humanity. It seeks to strike a balance between the potential of advanced technology and the core human needs that shape a just and thriving society.

1. Morals:

The moral framework of this system is centered around *responsibility*—to both individuals and the planet, acknowledging that technological and economic progress must respect human dignity and environmental sustainability.

- **Responsibility to Humanity:** The progress of technology, space exploration, and economic growth should be pursued with the primary aim of improving the quality of life for all people, especially the most vulnerable.

- **Responsibility to Future Generations:** The system must prioritize long-term sustainability, ensuring that actions taken today don't jeopardize the opportunities of tomorrow. This means investing in solutions that benefit future generations and leave behind a habitable planet and thriving space civilizations.

- **Justice and Equity:** All individuals, regardless of their nationality, race, or social standing, should have equal access to the opportunities created by space exploration, technological advancements, and economic systems. This system values fairness and seeks to minimize disparities caused by structural inequalities.

- **Interdependence:** Recognizing the interconnectedness of global economies and societies, the moral outlook emphasizes mutual respect, cooperation, and a shared commitment to collective well-being. All stakeholders must work collaboratively, especially in international efforts such as space exploration and energy/resource management.

2. Core Values:

- **Innovation with Integrity:** While innovation is encouraged, it must be done with transparency, respect for privacy, and fairness. Technology should enhance human capacity, not undermine autonomy or create new systems of control.

- **Sustainability:** Both economic systems and technological advancements must focus on *sustainable* practices, ensuring minimal environmental impact and addressing issues like resource scarcity and ecological degradation. This includes promoting alternative energy, sustainable agriculture, and the responsible use of space resources.

- **Inclusivity:** The system values the involvement and benefit of all people in the global economy. Technologies like digital banking, AI, and automation should be used to close gaps in access to essential services, improve financial inclusion, and create new opportunities for those previously left behind. No one should be excluded from the benefits of progress.

- **Competition with Cooperation:** While competition can drive innovation, it should not come at the expense of cooperation. In this system, healthy competition drives advancement and improves efficiency, but cooperation—particularly on a global scale—is necessary for overcoming the significant challenges humanity faces, such as space colonization, food security, and climate change.

- **Meritocracy:** Individuals and organizations should be recognized and rewarded based on their tangible contributions to society. Efforts to solve problems such as resource distribution or advancing space exploration should be incentivized through clear meritocratic structures, ensuring that success is determined by skill, innovation, and results.

- **Respect for Autonomy:** Technology, particularly AI and robotics, should be used to empower individuals, not replace or control them. Personal autonomy, privacy, and freedom should be protected in all technological systems, with safeguards in place to ensure that technologies like AI do not infringe on individual rights.

3. Ethical Principles:

- **Ethical Technological Advancement:** As technology like AI, automation, and space exploration progresses, it must always be directed toward positive societal goals. This includes minimizing risks such as job displacement or unethical use of data, and ensuring that technological advancements don't widen societal divides or lead to a concentration of power in the hands of a few.

- **Global Cooperation and Governance:** International collaboration and governance must be ethical, transparent, and aimed at promoting peace and fairness across borders. While competitive spirit can drive progress, it should not be at the expense of global solidarity. Shared resources (like space or environmental assets) should be managed collectively for the benefit of all nations and peoples.

- **Economic Ethics:** The digital banking and financial systems must be designed to eliminate inefficiencies, prevent exploitation, and foster long-term growth. Fair lending practices, ethical use of data, and creating equal access to financial opportunities are core to the ethical foundation of this system.

- **Human-Centric Decision-Making:** In all decisions—economic, technological, or political—the system should always prioritize human well-being. This includes addressing issues like overpopulation, economic inequality, and resource scarcity, ensuring that the needs of all individuals are considered as part of the broader vision.

- **Education and Knowledge Sharing:** For this system to succeed, education plays a critical role. The system must value universal access to high-quality education, particularly in science, technology, and ethics, to ensure that future generations are equipped to navigate the complexities of a rapidly changing world. Ethical education should also promote critical thinking, social responsibility, and the ability to act for the common good.

4. Practical Implementation Considerations:

- **Public-Private Partnerships:** Ensuring the successful application of these ideals requires collaboration between governments, businesses, and NGOs. Public and private sectors must work together to ensure that space exploration, technological advancements, and economic systems benefit all people equitably, and not just the wealthiest or most powerful nations.

- **Transparency and Accountability:** Every institution involved must operate transparently, with checks and balances in place to avoid corruption, manipulation, or inequity. Ethical guidelines and regulations should be clearly defined to guide companies and governments in their actions, particularly in industries like AI, space, and finance.

- **Cross-Cultural Sensitivity:** As this system calls for global cooperation, cultural differences should be acknowledged and respected. Ethical frameworks should be adaptable to diverse cultural and social norms, while still adhering to fundamental principles of human dignity, rights, and fairness.

5. Ethical Dilemmas and Resolutions:

- **Technological Unemployment:** As automation and AI disrupt traditional jobs, it's essential to create systems of retraining, universal basic income, or other social safety nets to ensure that displaced workers can transition into new roles and continue to contribute to society. The ethics of work in the digital age must prioritize human flourishing over pure economic efficiency.

- **Resource Allocation in Space:** The potential for space colonization to alleviate resource scarcity on Earth is promising, but ethical questions around resource extraction, environmental preservation, and the colonization of extraterrestrial bodies must be addressed. A space governance framework must be established to manage resources equitably and sustainably, avoiding the exploitation of new frontiers in the same way Earth's resources have been historically exploited.

This system of morals, values, and ethics is designed to guide the ambitious vision of modern economics, where technological progress, space exploration, and economic growth are balanced with human rights, sustainability, and global cooperation. By adhering to these principles, the vision can evolve into a better future for all, ensuring that advancements benefit humanity as a

whole while upholding justice, equity, and
responsibility.

Chapter 15: Economics of Nuclear Energy

The economics of nuclear energy ties into this vision by playing a key role in addressing some of humanity's most pressing challenges, especially resource scarcity and overpopulation. Nuclear energy, as a low-carbon, high-output power source, could serve as a cornerstone for both the technological advancements and sustainable economic models you're envisioning.

Here's how it relates to the different aspects of the paragraph:

1. **Resource Scarcity**: One of the core issues humanity faces today is the depletion of traditional energy sources, particularly fossil fuels, and the environmental damage they cause. Nuclear energy offers a potential solution by providing a vast amount of energy from relatively small amounts of fuel. It could help reduce dependence on dwindling natural resources while avoiding the harmful impacts of climate change. In a future where space exploration and colonization may play a role, nuclear power could be essential for the energy needs of off-planet missions and colonies. For example, nuclear reactors could power deep-space travel or provide stable, long-term energy supplies to lunar or Martian colonies.

2. **Economic Growth through Technological Advancements**: The comparison to the "Age of Exploration" in your paragraph is apt—just as that era sparked advancements in navigation, science, and trade, space exploration could drive innovations in technology. Nuclear energy fits into this

framework, as advancements in nuclear technologies (like smaller, safer reactors or fusion power) could accelerate technological progress. These breakthroughs could not only improve energy production on Earth but could also make space exploration more feasible by offering a compact, high-efficiency energy solution for long-duration missions.

3. **Artificial Intelligence and Automation**: Your vision of merging technology with economics to reduce inefficiencies aligns with the potential of nuclear energy. With advancements in AI and robotics, the nuclear energy sector could become more efficient and cost-effective. Automation in nuclear power plants could streamline operations, reduce human error, and improve safety. AI could also be used to predict maintenance needs, optimize energy output, and even aid in the design of next-generation nuclear reactors, such as small modular reactors (SMRs) or fusion reactors.

4. **Energy and Food Crises**: Addressing the energy crisis is directly tied to ensuring sustainable food production. Reliable, large-scale energy sources like nuclear power could enable the development of more energy-intensive agricultural technologies, such as vertical farming or advanced hydroponic systems, which would help feed the growing global population. Additionally, by solving the energy crisis, nuclear power could support other critical sectors like desalination and industrial processes needed

for food and water production in resource-scarce regions.

5. **Space Exploration**: Nuclear energy could play a pivotal role in powering space exploration efforts. For deep-space missions or the establishment of human habitats on the Moon or Mars, solar power alone is insufficient due to the vast distances and lack of sunlight in certain areas. Nuclear reactors could provide a continuous, stable source of energy for these missions. The development of space-based nuclear power also ties into the broader economic vision of resource expansion into space, where mining asteroids for resources and creating off-planet industries could benefit from nuclear energy's high energy density.

6. **Meritocratic Society and Competition**: A future that fosters competition, innovation, and meritocracy would benefit from advances in nuclear energy, particularly if the sector evolves in a way that opens up new opportunities for global investment and collaboration. The development of cleaner, safer nuclear technologies could create competitive industries where nations and private companies strive to innovate in energy production and space exploration. The space race could serve as an analogy for how competition can drive social progress, both in terms of technological advancements and in the democratization of energy access worldwide.

7. **Global Collaboration and Investment**: Just as the vision of a modern economy

requires international collaboration and investment, so does the advancement of nuclear energy. Building the infrastructure for nuclear energy at a global scale—whether for power generation or space exploration—would require cooperation between nations, shared knowledge, and substantial financial investment. International treaties, safety standards, and investment in education and workforce development would all be crucial in ensuring that nuclear energy can be harnessed safely and efficiently for the collective benefit of humanity.

In summary, nuclear energy could play a central role in powering the future you describe: a world driven by space exploration, technological innovation, and sustainable economic growth. By addressing energy challenges, contributing to economic efficiency, and enabling space exploration, nuclear power could be a key enabler of a future where technology and economics are deeply intertwined to solve humanity's biggest challenges.

To delve deeper into the economics of nuclear energy and how it relates to the vision of space exploration, economic systems, and societal progress, let's break this down with specific examples, statistics, and some economic and mathematical considerations.

1. Resource Scarcity and Energy Needs

As the world faces increasing energy demand and depleting fossil fuel reserves, nuclear energy stands as a viable solution for long-term sustainable energy. Here's how it fits into the broader economic framework:

- **Global Energy Demand**: According to the **International Energy Agency (IEA)**, global energy demand is expected to grow by 30% between 2020 and 2040. Meeting this demand will require a massive expansion of energy infrastructure.

- **Nuclear Energy's Role**: Nuclear energy currently provides around 10% of the world's electricity, but its potential could be far greater. For example:

  - **France** produces about 70% of its electricity from nuclear, which is an outstanding example of how nuclear can be scaled to meet significant energy needs.

  - **Small Modular Reactors (SMRs)**: A developing technology that promises lower construction costs and enhanced safety features. A report from **World Nuclear Association** suggests that SMRs could reduce the cost of nuclear plants by up to 30-50% compared to traditional large reactors.

  - **Fusion Power**: While still in its infancy, fusion could revolutionize energy production. The **International Thermonuclear Experimental Reactor (ITER)**, currently under construction in France, aims to demonstrate that fusion can be a viable energy source.

ITER's projected cost is around $22 billion, but successful demonstration could unlock fusion energy, which offers almost unlimited power using fuel derived from water (deuterium and tritium).

In terms of economics, nuclear energy is capital-intensive upfront but offers low operating costs. For example:

- The **levelized cost of energy (LCOE)** for nuclear power, according to a **2019 IEA report**, ranges from **$50 to $130 per megawatt-hour (MWh)**, depending on the location and technology used.

- **Nuclear Power Plant Capital Costs**: The initial construction cost for a traditional nuclear plant can be around **$6 billion to $9 billion**, and it may take 5-10 years to complete. While high, the long-term operational lifespan (40-60 years) and low operational costs make it competitive, especially as countries shift toward decarbonization goals.

2. Space Exploration as a Driver of Technological Advancement and Economic Growth

The vision of space exploration driving economic growth ties in directly with nuclear power for a few reasons:

- **Energy Needs in Space Exploration**: For extended space missions or colonization (e.g., on the Moon or Mars), nuclear energy is the most promising energy source due to its high energy density and reliability.

- A **nuclear thermal rocket (NTR)**, under development by NASA, could provide the necessary propulsion for missions to Mars by utilizing nuclear fission for more efficient propulsion than chemical rockets. An example of this is the **Kilopower project**, which aims to develop small fission reactors for deep space missions. NASA estimates that the cost of building a Kilopower reactor could be around **$30 million** per unit.

- **Moon and Mars Colonies**: Both NASA and private companies like **SpaceX** plan for human presence on the Moon and Mars. These colonies will require consistent energy supplies, for everything from life support to industrial processes. Nuclear energy's ability to provide consistent, on-demand power, regardless of local solar conditions, makes it the ideal solution.

For instance, the **Mars Society** and **NASA** are exploring how nuclear power could be used to provide energy for habitats, growing food, and water processing. These technologies will be capital-intensive but could generate returns in the form of new industries and the ability to harvest resources in space.

3. Technological Integration and Automation

The integration of artificial intelligence (AI), automation, and robotics with nuclear energy could significantly reduce inefficiencies and improve economic outcomes:

- **AI in Nuclear Power**: AI can help optimize nuclear plant operations, manage resources more efficiently, and predict maintenance needs, reducing downtime and increasing output. In a study published in **Nature Communications**, AI models have been shown to improve operational efficiencies by up to **10%** in energy plants.

- **Automation**: The nuclear industry has already started automating tasks that were previously done manually. **Robotics** are used for routine maintenance, reactor inspections, and waste management. The **Nuclear Robotics Program** has deployed robotic systems in places like Fukushima, where human intervention was too dangerous. These advancements lower operational costs and risks.

4. Solving the Energy and Food Crises

Energy and food crises are interlinked. Energy is required for agriculture, and nuclear energy could provide a solution by powering modern agricultural technologies:

- **Vertical Farming**: This high-tech farming approach requires energy for lighting, temperature control, and water management. For example, **vertical farms** in the U.S. use around **10 times more energy** than traditional farming. If nuclear energy were used, these farms could be powered with low-cost, low-emission energy.

- **Desalination**: Nuclear power could play a significant role in providing fresh water to arid regions through **desalination**. According to the **International Atomic Energy Agency (IAEA)**, nuclear power plants can be paired with desalination facilities to produce both power and water at a cost-effective rate. The **Kashiwazaki-Kariwa Nuclear Power Plant** in Japan has demonstrated this integration by producing both electricity and desalinated water.

- **Fusion and Food Security**: Long-term fusion energy development could provide energy for technologies like **synthetic biology** or **lab-grown meat**, both of which could address food shortages by enabling efficient, sustainable food production without the need for large-scale agriculture.

5. Economic and Societal Integration

Nuclear energy also ties into broader economic systems, including financial inclusion and societal values:

- **Global Finance and Inclusion**: The integration of energy systems with digital finance and automation (like the **Universal iPad/phone concept** mentioned in your paragraph) could allow for more equitable access to energy resources. Blockchain technology, for example, can enable decentralized energy trading, where nuclear energy producers could sell energy credits or excess energy to global markets. This opens up a new financial model that could be more efficient and inclusive.

- **Costs of Safety and Regulation**: One of the challenges of nuclear energy is ensuring safety while keeping costs manageable. According to the **World Nuclear Association**, regulatory frameworks are expensive, with costs for nuclear safety regulation accounting for **10-15%** of total plant construction costs. Overcoming these regulatory hurdles, while ensuring safety, would be necessary for the broader adoption of nuclear power on Earth and in space.

- The higher upfront cost, plus the complexity of operating in space, means nuclear may be the cheaper long-term solution for space exploration.

Conclusion

Incorporating nuclear energy into the futuristic economic vision outlined above—especially concerning space exploration, resource scarcity, and technological innovation—requires large investments upfront but promises substantial long-term returns in energy, technological progress, and even economic growth. With nuclear's high energy density, scalability, and potential for integration with advanced technologies like AI and robotics, it could be central to overcoming both Earth-bound and extraterrestrial energy challenges, enabling humanity to move beyond current limitations and toward a sustainable, technologically advanced future.

Chapter 16: Food and Nutrition

Chapter: Food and Nutrition in the Modern Economy

In the vision of a future economy that blends technological progress, space exploration, and sustainable development, food and nutrition emerge as central pillars. As we stand on the precipice of transformative advancements in technology, healthcare, and the global economy, addressing the challenges of food production and distribution is more urgent than ever. With the specter of overpopulation, resource scarcity, and the looming threat of climate change, food systems must evolve to meet the demands of a growing global population. Simultaneously, as we look toward the stars, space colonization offers the possibility of new agricultural frontiers, further extending our reach in the quest for sustainable food solutions.

The Intersection of Technology and Food Production

As automation, artificial intelligence, and robotics reshape economies across sectors, the agricultural landscape is also ripe for transformation. The future of food production will likely be characterized by highly efficient, automated farming systems, with technologies like vertical farming, precision agriculture, and genetically modified crops at the forefront. These innovations will aim to address the inefficiencies inherent in traditional farming methods, which consume enormous amounts of land, water, and labor. By combining machine learning with real-time data analytics, farms will be able to predict crop yields, optimize resource usage, and mitigate environmental damage, creating a more sustainable and scalable agricultural model.

Vertical farming, which involves growing crops in stacked layers, could revolutionize urban food production. By harnessing artificial intelligence and robotics, these urban farms could operate with minimal human intervention, dramatically reducing the carbon footprint of food production and distribution. Additionally, the controlled environment of vertical farms can reduce the need for pesticides and herbicides, creating healthier, more sustainable food options for communities.

Meanwhile, genetically modified organisms (GMOs) have the potential to solve some of the most pressing agricultural challenges, such as drought resistance, pest resistance, and increased nutritional value. Advanced gene editing tools, such as CRISPR, can allow for more precise modifications, leading to crops that are not only more resilient but also packed with essential nutrients. For example, biofortified crops could be engineered to address micronutrient deficiencies that affect billions of people globally, a critical issue in developing countries where malnutrition remains prevalent.

The Role of Space Exploration in Agricultural Innovation

One of the most exciting prospects of space exploration is its potential to drive innovations in agriculture that will have profound effects on food production on Earth. As humans explore the possibility of colonizing other planets, we will need to develop entirely new ways to grow food in extraterrestrial environments. This challenge could inspire breakthroughs in food technology that can be applied to Earth's resource-constrained settings.

The unique conditions of space—low gravity, extreme temperatures, and limited resources—will force scientists to rethink traditional agricultural practices. Innovations such as hydroponics, aquaponics, and aeroponics, all of which allow plants to grow without soil, could be refined for use in space habitats. These methods, already being tested on Earth, could become central to the future of farming, both in space and on Earth. By using less water and no soil, these systems offer solutions to some of the most pressing challenges in agriculture, such as soil degradation and water scarcity.

Moreover, space missions can lead to the development of closed-loop systems where food production, waste management, and resource consumption are interconnected and optimized for sustainability. If these systems prove successful on Mars or the Moon, they could be replicated on Earth, particularly in arid or resource-poor regions, creating new opportunities for sustainable food production in places where traditional farming is not feasible.

A Universal Digital Economy and Food Distribution

In tandem with these agricultural advancements, the rise of a global digital economy—enabled by technologies like blockchain, digital banking systems, and artificial intelligence—can transform food distribution and access. As we move toward a universal platform for digital transactions, we can imagine a world where food security is no longer constrained by geography or economic barriers. Digital platforms could provide equitable access to food, reducing waste, improving supply chains, and allowing for real-time tracking of food products from farm to table.

Through blockchain technology, we can create transparent, secure food supply chains that reduce fraud and ensure that food produced ethically and sustainably reaches consumers. Smart contracts could enable farmers, suppliers, and retailers to engage in fair transactions, while artificial intelligence could predict demand and adjust production levels accordingly, reducing food waste and ensuring that no one goes hungry.

A digital economy could also revolutionize food access for people in underserved regions. By connecting remote farmers to global markets, local food producers could earn fair compensation for their goods, while consumers would have access to more diverse, nutritious food options. Furthermore, digital platforms could support personalized nutrition by using artificial intelligence to provide individuals with customized dietary recommendations based on their health needs, preferences, and even genetic makeup.

Sustainability and the Future of Nutrition

The future of food is not just about quantity; it is also about quality. As global economic systems adapt to new technological realities, nutrition must be a central focus. The concept of a meritocratic society, as envisioned in The Modern Economy, must include not only access to adequate food but access to healthy, nutritious food that supports the well-being of individuals and communities. This is particularly important in a world where processed foods are becoming more ubiquitous, and chronic diseases like obesity, diabetes, and heart disease are on the rise.

Sustainable and nutritious food systems will need to take into account both the environmental impact of food production and the health benefits of what is consumed. A shift toward plant-based diets, which have lower carbon footprints than meat-heavy diets, could play a significant role in reducing greenhouse gas emissions. In addition, innovations in food technology, such as lab-grown meat and plant-based alternatives, could provide high-quality protein sources without the environmental cost associated with traditional animal agriculture.

The food of the future may also be enriched with nutrients that promote health and prevent disease. Advances in biotechnology could lead to personalized nutrition, where food is tailored not only to an individual's dietary needs but also to their genetic makeup. Imagine a world where genetic profiling helps people optimize their diets, improving their health and longevity while reducing the strain on healthcare systems.

Global Collaboration and Education for a Healthier Future

Achieving these ambitious goals requires global collaboration and significant investment in education, infrastructure, and technology. The agricultural innovations necessary to feed the world's growing population will require investment in research and development, as well as international cooperation to ensure that the benefits are shared equitably. This collaboration will extend beyond borders and sectors, bringing together governments, businesses, and communities to tackle food insecurity, malnutrition, and sustainability on a global scale.

At the same time, education will be key in shaping a future where both food production and consumption align with sustainability and health. As the global population becomes more connected through digital platforms, it is crucial that individuals understand the implications of their food choices, not only for their health but also for the planet. The rise of digital education platforms and the integration of sustainability and nutrition into curricula could foster a generation of individuals who are more mindful of their food choices and the impact those choices have on the world.

Conclusion: A Vision for the Future

The future of food and nutrition in the context of a rapidly evolving economy is one of transformation and possibility. By leveraging the power of technology, space exploration, and a universal digital economy, we can create food systems that are more efficient, equitable, and sustainable. As we move toward this new frontier, it is essential that we balance innovation with humanity's fundamental needs, ensuring that everyone—regardless of their geographic location or economic status—has access to the nutritious food they need to thrive. This ambitious vision holds the promise of not just feeding the world, but nourishing it in ways that foster both individual well-being and global sustainability.

The Synergy Between Space Resources and Earth-Based Agriculture

As humanity expands into space, we are likely to see a growing synergy between extraterrestrial resource exploration and terrestrial agricultural systems. Beyond the immediate necessity of growing food in space, the technologies developed for space habitats could be leveraged to address Earth's pressing challenges. For instance, advancements in mining asteroids for water and minerals could provide new resources for farming innovations on Earth. Space missions designed to extract and refine resources like water or carbon dioxide from other planets could have direct applications in agricultural systems on Earth, aiding in water-scarce regions or even boosting crop yields in areas affected by climate change.

Imagine a scenario where mining asteroids provides rare minerals that are essential for soil enrichment, enhancing global agricultural productivity. Additionally, the advances made in space-based energy production, such as solar harvesting in space, could bring sustainable energy solutions to Earth, fueling energy-intensive food production systems, like vertical farms, while reducing their carbon footprints.

Closing the Nutritional Gap with Personalized Food Technology

Looking beyond traditional methods of growing and distributing food, personalized food technology could become a game changer in addressing global nutritional disparities. Rather than simply focusing on increasing the quantity of food available, the focus could shift toward enhancing the nutritional quality tailored to individuals' specific needs. This approach would require advances in genomics, biotechnology, and AI to understand the nutritional needs of each person based on factors like their genetic predispositions, health conditions, and lifestyle.

In the future, a person's daily nutritional intake might be managed through an automated system, possibly connected to a universal digital platform that monitors their dietary intake in real-time. Such a system would ensure that everyone—regardless of income level—has access to food that meets their individual health needs. This could involve personalized food supplements, 3D-printed meals, or even bioengineered food products designed to combat specific health challenges like vitamin deficiencies or chronic diseases.

The rise of synthetic biology and lab-grown foods could further refine this approach, allowing us to produce not only more nutrient-dense foods but also ones that are more palatable and culturally tailored. With advances in fermentation technologies, proteins such as algae, fungi, and yeast can be grown in controlled environments, offering high-quality protein sources that are both sustainable and nutritionally rich. These technologies could reduce dependency on traditional livestock farming, which is resource-intensive and often environmentally damaging.

Urban Agriculture and Global Food Security

The growth of urban populations and the challenges of feeding them have sparked a renewed focus on urban agriculture. As cities become more densely populated, traditional food systems based on rural farming and long-distance transportation are becoming less viable. Urban agriculture—using technologies like hydroponics, aquaponics, and urban rooftop farming—could provide cities with locally produced, fresh food. These systems will be particularly useful in densely populated regions where arable land is limited or where the environmental footprint of transportation needs to be minimized.

These urban farming systems could rely on closed-loop ecosystems, powered by renewable energy sources and waste recovery technologies. Urban agriculture can also be more resilient to climate change, providing food security even in the face of unpredictable weather patterns that impact rural farming. By utilizing AI to predict climate patterns and optimize growth conditions, urban farms could scale rapidly, providing affordable and nutritious food to millions in cities around the world.

This approach also shifts the traditional model of food distribution, reducing reliance on centralized food hubs and global supply chains. Instead, cities could become self-sustaining food ecosystems, reducing food waste and fostering local food sovereignty. However, this transition would need significant investments in infrastructure, education, and policy to ensure equitable access to these resources across all socioeconomic strata.

The Role of Education and Public Awareness

As food production evolves, so too must our understanding of nutrition. Education will play a critical role in shaping a future where people are not only healthier but more attuned to the environmental and economic impacts of their food choices. A future economy that integrates technology into every aspect of life should also ensure that nutritional literacy becomes as fundamental as financial literacy.

Public awareness campaigns, digital platforms, and school curricula focused on sustainable and healthy eating could help shift consumption patterns toward plant-based, nutrient-dense diets. Education about the environmental footprint of food, along with the cultural and ethical considerations of food choices, would support a more conscious society. As the digital economy grows, food systems may also become more transparent. Blockchain could allow consumers to trace the origin of their food and understand its impact on both the environment and their health.

Moreover, governments and private sectors could partner to develop programs that address food deserts—areas where access to fresh produce and healthy foods is limited—by implementing technology-driven solutions. These solutions could involve mobile markets, food distribution apps, and local processing facilities that enable access to healthy food in remote or underserved regions.

A Global Food System for a More Equitable Future

A key challenge in shaping the future of food is ensuring that technological advancements do not perpetuate existing inequalities. A truly global food system needs to be equitable, addressing not just the nutritional needs of the wealthy but also those of the most vulnerable populations. The innovations in food production, distribution, and access must be designed with inclusivity in mind.

This could involve scaling up sustainable agricultural methods in developing regions, providing smallholder farmers with access to digital tools that optimize crop production, or offering low-cost, high-nutrient food options to impoverished communities. Financial inclusion—through platforms like universal digital banking systems—could allow marginalized communities to access capital, invest in farming technologies, and connect with global food markets, improving local food security while stimulating economic growth.

International cooperation will be critical to this effort. A future economy that thrives on collaboration, rather than competition, can support food systems that benefit all nations, regardless of their economic standing. Global treaties could set standards for food production that prioritize sustainability, fairness, and human dignity, ensuring that no one is left behind in the quest for nutritious, sustainable food.

The original economy was hunting and gathering, which then transitioned into subsistence agriculture, which led into industrial economies and then service economies. Economists believe that service economies are the most advanced form. It seems that key economic factors were lost in translation during the transitions society had to undertake. Modern economics is about filling those gaps, learning from past mistakes, and developing a market that is more efficient. How can our needs be met in a capitalistic society, if so much is deferred to the cultivation of raw materials. Resources need to be more efficiently allocated and distributed. Modern economics should seek applications to satisfy those needs. Technology should be applied appropriately to accomplish those goals where society sees fit. The developing world has experienced its fair share of food shortage and famine. So much goes into the preparation, cultivation, and processing of food. We can increase our agricultural production by planting the food that comes from overseas in our very own backyards. We no longer need lawn mowers. Let it grow. If food output increases, we can reduce the costs associated with the food industry. This will cause a demand for low skill labor and might help decrease the unemployment rate. Being modern so to speak is about being practical. This is a doable profit seeking business model that will allow service economies to integrate such an initiative into daily life. This is better than an urban renewal project because food is more important than shelter. When food supply increases, we can expect increases in demand as well. This market is healthy for nations looking to improve production and consumption. The "Modern Economic Food Program" will eliminate unnecessary logistical problems, reduce shipping costs, and support local produce. We are reviving subsistence agricultural through basic service industries. I guess you could say a food revolution would pay homage to fundamental human needs. Most products and service are designed to make life easier. The further we deviate from the need for food shelter and water, the more costly things become. And, more complicated. Doesn't this defeat its own purpose?

Subsistence Agriculture – Reimagining the Economic Model

The progression of human economies has followed a series of stages, each influenced by the prevailing technological and social developments of the time. Initially, societies were based on **hunting and gathering**, where communities relied on nature's bounty for sustenance. As populations grew, the next step was the advent of **subsistence agriculture** — individuals and communities began to produce food primarily for their own consumption, using simple tools and techniques. This shift enabled human settlements to flourish, marking the beginning of **agrarian economies**. Over time, however, technological advances spurred the growth of **industrial economies**, and later, the rise of the **service economy**, where many individuals work in non-manufacturing sectors, such as retail, finance, or healthcare.

While service economies are often seen as the peak of economic sophistication, they carry with them certain challenges that may have been overlooked in the historical transitions from agriculture to industrialization. One crucial gap is the growing disconnection from the fundamental resources and systems that sustain life, namely food, water, and shelter. The shift from subsistence agriculture to industrialization has created a reliance on complex global supply chains and massive infrastructure that are often inefficient and unsustainable.

In the modern economic landscape, much of the world's agricultural production is outsourced to regions with lower labor costs, creating supply chains that are susceptible to disruption. Global food shortages, famines, and significant environmental consequences have highlighted the need for more localized, sustainable solutions. **The question remains: How can we meet our basic needs for food in a world that has become increasingly disconnected from these core human requirements?** The answer lies in **revisiting subsistence agriculture**, leveraging modern tools and technologies to scale it in ways that meet both the economic and social needs of contemporary societies.

1. The Inefficiency of Global Supply Chains:

The production and distribution of food have become increasingly complex and globalized. For instance, much of the food consumed in developed countries is grown in far-off regions. This reliance on imports comes with significant costs:

- **Shipping costs**: Transporting food from one part of the world to another involves significant logistical expenses. For example, transporting avocados from Mexico to the U.S. adds up not just in cost but also in carbon emissions.

- **Food waste**: A large portion of food produced globally is wasted due to inefficiencies in the supply chain, including spoilage during long-distance transportation or due to complex packaging processes.
- **Unpredictable supply disruptions**: Events like natural disasters, political instability, or pandemics can disrupt international supply chains, as seen in the 2020 COVID-19 pandemic, which resulted in widespread food shortages and price inflation in many parts of the world.

Revisiting **subsistence agriculture** — growing food in one's own backyard or local community — can mitigate these inefficiencies. With advances in technology, growing food locally can reduce dependence on far-flung supply chains, lower the carbon footprint of food production, and make communities more resilient to supply shocks.

2. Localizing Food Production through Technology:

Modern technologies have made subsistence agriculture more feasible than ever. Urban farming, vertical farming, hydroponics, and even backyard greenhouses enable individuals and communities to grow food on small plots of land, reducing the need for large-scale industrial agriculture. For example:

- **Hydroponic systems** allow for the cultivation of food in areas where traditional farming is not possible, such as arid regions or urban spaces with limited land. Companies like **AeroFarms** are pioneering vertical farming solutions that maximize crop yields per square foot using less water and space than conventional farming methods.
- **Urban agriculture initiatives** have been successful in major cities around the world,

such as **Detroit** and **London**, where individuals or cooperatives convert vacant urban land into spaces for growing fruits and vegetables.

- **Smart farming technologies**, like **IoT sensors** and **drones**, help monitor plant health, manage water usage, and optimize fertilizer application, significantly increasing the efficiency of small-scale farming efforts.

By making such technologies widely available, we could encourage more urban dwellers to take up small-scale food production, easing the strain on global food supply chains and improving local food security.

3. Practical Implications for Modern Economies:

Subsistence agriculture, when applied on a larger scale, can play a pivotal role in meeting food needs while also stimulating economic growth. The growth of local food systems could address several key economic challenges:

- **Reducing unemployment**: In the process of reviving subsistence agriculture, low-skilled jobs could be created, particularly in the developing world. Jobs like food production, local distribution, and food preparation could provide a new, stable source of income for those with limited access to formal education or skilled labor opportunities.
- **Revitalizing communities**: Communities engaged in local food production might see increased cohesion and collaboration. Urban gardens and local food cooperatives promote community-building, allowing individuals to share resources, knowledge, and labor.
- **Reducing the cost of food**: By cutting out the middlemen in food distribution, the cost

of food production could decrease. Small-scale local farms have the potential to offer fresh, affordable produce, lowering grocery store prices, especially in underserved areas where fresh food is often more expensive than processed alternatives.

4. The "Modern Economic Food Program":

This concept embodies the shift from a heavily industrialized food system to one that emphasizes **local, sustainable food production**. This initiative would:

- **Eliminate unnecessary logistical problems**: With food being grown locally, there is less need for complex logistics and transportation, reducing both costs and environmental impact.
- **Support local economies**: Rather than relying on multinational corporations for food distribution, local agricultural production supports regional economies by keeping money circulating within communities.
- **Encourage sustainability**: A focus on locally grown food encourages sustainable farming practices and minimizes the overexploitation of natural resources. It can also lead to innovations in agriculture that improve soil health, reduce water use, and protect biodiversity.

5. A New Model for Economic Growth:

By integrating subsistence agriculture back into the fabric of modern economies, we're not only addressing immediate needs but creating a system that's more sustainable and resilient. In this **new model of economic growth**, rather than seeing service economies as the pinnacle of development, societies can work to blend industrial, service, and subsistence agricultural systems. Here's why this is practical:

- **Basic needs are prioritized**: By focusing on what really matters — food, shelter, water — we can create a more balanced economy where these fundamental needs are met more efficiently, allowing society to focus on broader innovations.
- **Profit-seeking business models**: The development of local food production can also become profitable. Small businesses, such as community-supported agriculture (CSA) programs or local farmers' markets, can serve as thriving economic models while addressing the food needs of the population.
- **Increased demand for local produce**: As more people participate in local food production, demand for locally sourced, sustainable produce could rise. This could spur the creation of new food products, technologies, and services designed around local agricultural systems, thus providing more economic opportunities.

Conclusion:

Reviving **subsistence agriculture** through modern technology, community engagement, and sustainable practices offers a practical and profitable business model that can integrate with the needs of **modern service economies**. As the world faces increasing challenges related to food security, environmental sustainability, and economic inequality, looking to the past for solutions — while adapting them with the tools of today — could provide a roadmap for a more resilient and efficient economic future. By filling the gaps left by previous economic transitions and focusing on the most fundamental human needs, we can create a system that not only meets our current demands but also builds a strong foundation for future generations.

Here's an in-depth look at how **subsistence agriculture** could play a transformative role in modern economies, with examples to illustrate the concepts mentioned in the previous elaboration:

1. Reducing Dependence on Global Supply Chains

1. **AeroFarms** (USA) – A leader in vertical farming, using aeroponic technology to grow leafy greens indoors with minimal land and water.
2. **Detroit Black Community Food Security Network** (USA) – Revitalizes urban spaces by converting vacant lots into urban farms, offering local food production and a more resilient local economy.
3. **Agri-Tech East** (UK) – A network of agribusinesses that create smart farming solutions like IoT sensors and data analytics, helping small farms manage resources more effectively.
4. **Lufa Farms** (Canada) – Uses rooftops of buildings to create urban farms, producing local vegetables with fewer resources and lower costs.
5. **Food Forward** (USA) – This nonprofit gathers surplus food and distributes it locally, reducing reliance on large food supply chains and waste.

2. Localizing Food Production through Technology

6. **Gotham Greens** (USA) – Vertical farming company that grows produce on rooftops in cities like New York, drastically reducing transportation costs and environmental impact.
7. **Kimbal Musk's Square Roots** (USA) – Urban farming startup focused on local

production using modular, climate-controlled farming environments.

8. **Hydroponics** (global) – From urban centers to rural communities, hydroponic farming techniques allow for food production in areas that lack fertile soil or arable land.
9. **Urban Growers Collective** (USA) – Uses aquaponics to grow food in Chicago's urban environment while also training local communities in sustainable food production.
10. **The Greenhouse at Microsoft** (USA) – Microsoft's data center and its greenhouses combine data technology with farming, producing food for employees while using sustainable, low-energy methods.

3. Practical Implications for Modern Economies

11. **Modular Farms** (Global) – Modular farming systems, which can be implemented in urban areas, give individuals the tools to grow their food locally with fewer resources.
12. **Local Harvest** (USA) – An online platform for finding locally grown food from farmers and producers in your area, directly connecting consumers to food growers.
13. **Farmigo** (USA) – A digital platform that enables communities to set up local food cooperatives, allowing families to access fresh produce while supporting local farmers.
14. **Harlem Grown** (USA) – Focuses on providing food education and local, organic food options for underserved urban communities, empowering them to grow their own food.
15. **Rooftop Farming in Singapore** (Singapore) – Singapore is using its limited land space for rooftop farming initiatives like **Sky Greens**, which grows vegetables using vertical farming techniques.

4. Reducing the Cost of Food

16. **Farm-to-Table Programs** (USA/Global) –
By eliminating the middleman, local farmers
sell directly to consumers or restaurants,
reducing food costs and increasing
transparency.
17. **Local Food Hubs** (USA/Global) – Local
hubs where farmers can directly sell their
products to consumers, cutting out large
supply chains and ensuring better prices.
18. **CSAs (Community Supported
Agriculture)** (Global) – A model where
individuals subscribe to receive weekly or
monthly deliveries of fresh, locally grown
produce, bypassing traditional grocery store
markups.
19. **Substack Farms** (USA) – A newsletter for
farmers who wish to sell directly to
customers, keeping costs low while offering
fresh, locally grown food.
20. **Low-cost Farmers' Markets** (Global) – By
shopping at local farmers' markets,
consumers often pay less for fresh produce,
supporting local economies and reducing
shipping costs.

5. Revitalizing Communities

21. **Growing Power** (USA) – A community-
based urban farming initiative that not only
provides food but also educates youth in
underserved areas, teaching them
sustainable agricultural techniques.
22. **Alberta Urban Agricultural Society**
(Canada) – Promotes sustainable agriculture
in urban settings, revitalizing neglected
areas while teaching local residents about
farming.
23. **The Land Institute** (USA) – A nonprofit
organization that focuses on regenerating the
soil and community-based food systems.

24. **Kiss the Ground** (USA) – Nonprofit promoting regenerative agriculture and teaching communities about sustainable food production and soil health.
25. **West Oakland Food Collaborative** (USA) – A collective that promotes urban farming, educates the community, and provides access to healthy, locally grown food.

6. Fostering Sustainable Agriculture Practices

26. **Regenerative Agriculture** (Global) – Companies like **Nourish Matters** and **Farmers for Climate Action** are using regenerative farming methods to create more sustainable food production practices that heal the soil, sequester carbon, and support biodiversity.
27. **Permaculture Projects** (Global) – **The Permaculture Institute** is training farmers in sustainable techniques like agroforestry, natural pest control, and water management that build resilient food systems.
28. **Earthworks Farm** (USA) – A farm that uses sustainable practices to grow food in harmony with nature, emphasizing soil health and water conservation.
29. **Polyculture Farming** (Global) – Growing multiple crops together to improve soil health, biodiversity, and minimize the need for synthetic fertilizers and pesticides.
30. **Fair Trade Farming** (Global) – Companies like **Fair Trade USA** are promoting fair, ethical production methods for farmers worldwide, ensuring they receive fair wages and support.

7. Creating Sustainable Economic Opportunities

31. **The World Wildlife Fund (WWF) Sustainable Agriculture Program** (Global) – WWF collaborates with farmers and businesses to encourage sustainable farming practices and promote economic stability through eco-friendly methods.
32. **Cargill's Climate-Smart Agriculture Initiatives** (Global) – Cargill is investing in programs that teach farmers how to adopt climate-smart agriculture practices, benefiting local economies and the environment.
33. **Gaining Ground** (USA) – A nonprofit that provides affordable, organic produce to low-income communities while empowering local farmers to create viable, sustainable businesses.
34. **The Sustainable Agriculture Initiative Platform** (Global) – An organization bringing together food industry leaders to promote sustainable practices in the food value chain, improving both the environment and local economies.
35. **AgFunder** (Global) – An investment platform that connects agricultural technology startups with investors, helping create economic opportunities in food production and sustainable agriculture.

8. Addressing Unemployment through Local Agriculture

36. **Agri-Lending Programs** (India) – Programs like **NABARD** (National Bank for Agriculture and Rural Development) offer loans to farmers to boost local agricultural productivity, stimulating job growth in rural areas.
37. **Vertical Harvest** (USA) – A vertical farm in Wyoming that employs local people and trains them in sustainable agriculture techniques, helping reduce unemployment in the area.

38. **Food Security and Livelihoods Programs** (Kenya) – Programs like **Hivos** are teaching farmers how to implement sustainable farming techniques, providing jobs and combating food insecurity.
39. **Farm Corps** (USA) – A nonprofit offering youth employment in sustainable farming projects, equipping them with skills they can use for future employment.
40. **The Green Business Network** (USA) – Supports small businesses, including those in agriculture, to provide training, resources, and funding to create new jobs and boost economic opportunities in local communities.

9. Eliminating Logistical Problems

41. **GrubMarket** (USA) – This platform connects food producers directly to buyers (consumers and businesses), streamlining the supply chain and reducing unnecessary logistical expenses.
42. **Local Farm Co-ops** (Global) – Co-ops like **The Cooperative Grocer Network** in the U.S. allow farmers to pool resources, share costs, and reduce logistical inefficiencies.
43. **Good Food Accelerator** (USA) – Helps small-scale food entrepreneurs access business support, technical resources, and networks to scale their local food systems efficiently.
44. **Local Food Distributors** (Global) – Companies like **La Fresh** in India focus on connecting local farmers to direct markets, eliminating the need for expensive and complicated food distribution systems.
45. **Greenwave** (USA) – A nonprofit helping fishermen create sustainable, regenerative ocean farming practices to reduce the need for resource-intensive and costly supply chains.

10. Profit-Seeking Business Models in Food Production

46. **Sprouts Farmers Market** (USA) – A grocery chain focused on providing fresh, local produce at competitive prices, capitalizing on the growing demand for fresh, locally sourced food.
47. **Whole Foods Market** (USA) – The grocer has pushed the trend of selling locally grown food, creating a business model based on transparency, fresh produce, and sustainability.
48. **Patagonia Provisions** (USA) – An arm of Patagonia selling sustainable food products, showing how business can make a profit while promoting environmental sustainability and local food systems.
49. **Impossible Foods** (USA) – A company that produces plant-based meat alternatives with the goal of reducing the environmental impact of traditional meat production.
50. **Aldi's Local Sourcing Strategy** (Global) – Aldi has adopted a local-sourcing strategy for many of its food items, which cuts down on transportation costs, and supports local farmers and economies.

Conclusion:

These 50 examples show the significant shift possible in modern economies towards **subsistence agriculture** while leveraging technology to build efficient, local food systems. Whether it's through innovations in farming techniques, sustainable practices, or localized food production, societies can reduce their dependence on global supply chains, create more jobs, and ensure that basic needs are met in a sustainable and practical way.

Conclusion: A Holistic Vision for the Future of Food

In a future economy where space exploration, digital technologies, and sustainability intersect, food and nutrition will no longer be isolated challenges but central components of a broader vision for humanity's advancement. The next frontier in food production will be characterized by precision, sustainability, and inclusivity, all driven by a commitment to improving the well-being of individuals and the planet. By harnessing innovation across multiple sectors, we have the potential to create a food system that is not only capable of feeding the world but nourishing it in ways that support both human health and the health of our ecosystems.

Chapter 17: Universal Basic Income In The Modern Economy

Universal Basic Income (UBI) is a concept that proposes providing every individual with a regular, unconditional sum of money, regardless of employment status or economic standing. It's a progressive economic model aimed at ensuring that all people have access to a financial safety net, which would allow them to meet their basic needs and enjoy a baseline level of economic security. Unlike traditional welfare programs, UBI is not means-tested, and there are no work requirements, making it a universal solution designed to reduce poverty and inequality across society.

The idea of UBI addresses the growing disparities in wealth and opportunity that technology and globalization have exacerbated. As automation and artificial intelligence continue to disrupt labor markets, UBI offers a way to decouple income from traditional work. In a world where many jobs may no longer be sustainable, UBI could ensure that individuals still have the means to contribute to society, pursue education, or engage in creative and entrepreneurial activities.

This vision aligns closely with technological advancements, such as space exploration and the integration of AI in various sectors. With UBI, people would have the financial security to participate in these global initiatives, whether by working in innovative industries, engaging in educational opportunities, or contributing to large-scale projects like space colonization, without the immediate pressure of financial survival. It can also encourage people to invest in sustainable technologies or embrace new ways of living that are not dictated by economic necessity but by personal choice and societal progress.

Furthermore, UBI promotes financial inclusion by ensuring everyone has access to the economic system. This can be particularly impactful in regions where access to banking and financial services is limited. By leveraging modern digital infrastructure, such as smartphones and digital banking systems, UBI could be distributed efficiently, breaking down geographical and socio-economic barriers that have historically excluded large portions of the global population from economic opportunities.

In summary, Universal Basic Income is a transformative policy that addresses both the immediate and long-term challenges of modern economies. It empowers individuals to pursue a higher quality of life, fosters creativity and innovation, and ensures that technological and economic progress benefits all of humanity, not just the privileged few. Through its potential to offer financial stability in an increasingly automated world, UBI holds the promise of a more equitable and sustainable future.

In an era of rapid technological innovation, economic restructuring, and shifting societal paradigms, the concept of Universal Basic Income (UBI) emerges as both a bold and practical solution to a variety of global challenges. As outlined in the vision of modern economics, UBI ties directly into the overarching goals of creating a more inclusive, adaptable, and resilient global economy. It intersects with the ambition to explore new frontiers—be it through space exploration, technological progress, or resource management—by providing individuals with a financial foundation that frees them to contribute to these advancements without the constant burden of economic survival.

The Future of Space Exploration and Resource Scarcity

The idea of space exploration as a driving force for economic growth is undeniably compelling. Much like the "Age of Exploration," when human curiosity and ambition led to the expansion of trade networks and technological breakthroughs, space exploration promises to be the next great leap for humanity. Yet, as we aim to harness the vast resources of outer space, it is essential to recognize the economic and social implications of such endeavors.

UBI is inherently linked to this concept, providing a financial safety net that ensures every person can benefit from the economic fruits of space exploration. As humanity begins to colonize other planets and extract resources from asteroids or distant moons, the wealth generated from these ventures could be more widely distributed. Universal Income could act as a mechanism for ensuring that the wealth of space exploration is not confined to a select few but is shared broadly, addressing both the potential for overpopulation on Earth and the scarcity of resources.

In this new economic order, UBI could also serve as a way to alleviate societal stressors that arise from the disparities between those who control access to space resources and the general populace. With a guaranteed income, people would have the financial stability to pursue opportunities in the space industry, contribute to technological innovations, or simply improve their quality of life, whether on Earth or off-world.

The Role of Technology: AI, Automation, and Economic Efficiency

The integration of artificial intelligence, robotics, and automation into economic systems is reshaping the global workforce. From manufacturing to healthcare, technological advancements are steadily reducing the need for human labor in certain sectors, leading to concerns about mass unemployment and economic inequality. Yet, the fear that technology will eliminate jobs can be mitigated through the implementation of UBI.

In a world where artificial intelligence and automation increasingly drive productivity, UBI ensures that workers who are displaced by these technologies do not face destitution. Instead of relying on obsolete labor models, UBI would allow individuals to pursue more creative, intellectual, or entrepreneurial endeavors that could lead to the next wave of technological innovation. By decoupling income from traditional employment, UBI empowers people to engage with the economy in new and more meaningful ways, contributing to advancements in technology while being shielded from the economic upheavals that often accompany disruption.

Moreover, UBI could also address the inherent inefficiencies in traditional economic systems. With a digital banking infrastructure in place, as suggested in the vision, the distribution of UBI could be highly efficient, using algorithms and automation to optimize credit, trade, and lending systems. The very technologies that are transforming industries could also be harnessed to ensure that economic inclusion is not limited by geography, social status, or other barriers, creating a level playing field for all.

Economic Inclusion and Financial Empowerment

The concept of a universal digital banking system—enabled through devices like a universal iPad or phone—aligns directly with UBI in promoting financial inclusion. Access to digital financial systems has the potential to break down the geographical and socio-economic barriers that have historically prevented large swathes of the global population from participating fully in the economy.

In many parts of the world, people are excluded from the traditional banking system, either due to lack of infrastructure, identity verification issues, or financial illiteracy. With a universally connected device and the digital currency or financial system tied to UBI, these barriers can be dismantled. By ensuring that everyone, regardless of location or economic status, has access to the financial tools necessary to thrive, UBI promotes a truly global economy, where opportunities for prosperity are more equally distributed.

Moreover, financial empowerment through UBI allows individuals to engage more deeply with the economy, whether by starting businesses, investing in their education, or contributing to new innovations. As technology reduces costs and increases productivity, UBI provides a consistent stream of income to individuals, allowing them to experiment and innovate without the immediate fear of financial collapse.

Addressing Global Challenges: Energy, Food, and Sustainability

The vision of leveraging technology to address critical global challenges—such as energy and food scarcity—can only succeed if economic systems support the necessary investments in infrastructure, innovation, and human capital. UBI is not just a financial tool but a foundational component in supporting sustainable growth.

In the context of food and energy crises, UBI can help ensure that investments in sustainable practices and green technologies are not hindered by the immediate financial struggles of individuals or governments. People who receive a guaranteed income may be more inclined to adopt sustainable practices, invest in renewable energy, or pursue careers in green technology, all of which contribute to addressing long-term ecological challenges.

Additionally, the concept of space exploration and the extraction of resources from other planets or moons requires extensive collaboration and international cooperation. By ensuring a basic level of financial security for individuals globally, UBI could foster a more united effort to solve these problems. If people are less preoccupied with basic survival, they are better positioned to contribute to large-scale global projects that prioritize sustainability, technological development, and the long-term health of the planet.

Creating a Meritocratic Society: Rewarding Results

A meritocratic society rewards individuals based on their contributions, innovations, and results. As the vision suggests, space exploration and technological innovation could serve as metaphors for broader societal progress. UBI aligns with this meritocratic ideal by ensuring that everyone has an opportunity to contribute based on their talents and aspirations, not their financial status or access to traditional forms of labor.

Through UBI, people can choose to pursue careers in fields that align with their strengths, passions, and values, rather than being forced into low-wage or undesirable jobs due to financial necessity. This freedom to explore, innovate, and contribute to society in a meaningful way leads to a more dynamic, creative, and results-oriented economy.

Challenges and Implementation

Despite its potential, the implementation of UBI is not without its challenges. Political resistance, concerns over funding, and logistical hurdles must be overcome for UBI to become a reality. However, as the vision of modern economics emphasizes, these challenges are not insurmountable. They require careful planning, international collaboration, and significant investment in infrastructure, education, and technology.

The key to success lies in aligning the interests of various stakeholders—governments, corporations, and individuals—toward a shared vision of prosperity, sustainability, and equity. As technological advances continue to transform the global economy, UBI could serve as a necessary counterbalance, ensuring that the benefits of progress are widely shared, not just concentrated in the hands of a few.

In conclusion, Universal Basic Income is more than just a financial policy. It is a fundamental piece of a larger vision for a future where technology, space exploration, and economic innovation are harnessed to create a more inclusive, sustainable, and meritocratic society. By addressing humanity's core challenges—resource scarcity, overpopulation, and inequality—UBI has the potential to empower individuals, stimulate creativity, and ensure that the benefits of progress are enjoyed by all.